Alexander Ireland

In memoriam. Ralph Waldo Emerson

Recollections of his visits to England in 1833, 1847-8, 1872-3, and extracts from

unpublished letters

Alexander Ireland

In memoriam. Ralph Waldo Emerson
Recollections of his visits to England in 1833, 1847-8, 1872-3, and extracts from unpublished letters

ISBN/EAN: 9783743328457

Manufactured in Europe, USA, Canada, Australia, Japa

Cover: Foto ©ninafisch / pixelio.de

Manufactured and distributed by brebook publishing software
(www.brebook.com)

Alexander Ireland

In memoriam. Ralph Waldo Emerson

RALPH WALDO EMERSON.

THE grave has scarcely closed over the remains of the great man whose renown all over the world is more firmly established than that of any Englishman of his time, when the news comes to us that the foremost thinker and philosopher of America has joined the ranks of the majority. America has produced great soldiers, distinguished men of science, and poets of world-wide fame, but it is not too much to say that since the Declaration of Independence no man has so powerfully influenced the intellect of the nation as Ralph Waldo Emerson. On Thursday night, April 27th, at nine o'clock, at his house in Concord, Mass., surrounded by those dearest to him, this great man peaceably departed. He leaves a widow, a son—Dr. Edward Emerson, of Concord,—and two daughters. The eldest, Ellen—who was his tender and faithful companion whenever he left home, his amanuensis in his later years, and, as he sometimes lovingly called her, his "memory"—is unmarried. The youngest, Edith, is married to Colonel W. H. Forbes, of Milton Hill, Mass., and has a numerous family. When they visited England in 1872, bringing their children with them, Mr. Carlyle sat for a likeness, with Emerson's grandson, Ralph, then a fine boy of twelve or thirteen, standing by his knee.

Ralph Waldo Emerson, the most original and independent thinker and greatest moral teacher that America has produced, was born at Boston in 1803. He was a legitimate product of Puritanism. As far back as his family is traced it has been represented by ministers of the old faith of New England, the founder of it having journeyed thither with his congregation from Gloucestershire, in England, in 1635, and each of these ministers was associated with some phase of that faith, whether Calvinism, Universalism, or Unitarianism. His ancestry on both sides forms an indispensable explanation and background of every page of his writings. The Emerson family were intellectual, eloquent, with a strong individuality of character, robust and vigorous in their thinking—practical and philanthropic. His father was the Rev. William Emerson, pastor of the First (Unitarian) Church of Boston, and was noted for his vigorous mind, earnestness of purpose, and gentleness of manner. The boy lost his father when he was but eight years old. His mother was a woman of great sensibility, modest, serene, and very devout. "She was possessed of a thoroughly sincere nature, devoid of all sentimentalism, and of a temper the most even and placid—(one of her sons said that in his boyhood, when she came from her room in the morning, it seemed to him as if she always came from communion with God)—knew how to guide the affairs of her house, had the sweetest authority, and manners of natural grace and dignity. Her dark, liquid eyes, from which old age did not take away the expression, were among the remembrances of all on whom they ever rested." The young Emerson was very carefully educated, and entered Harvard University at an early age, where he graduated in 1821. Every graduating class in that institution elects a poet and an orator for its celebration, which is called "class-day," and Emerson was chosen as the poet of his class. In his junior year he received a Bowdoin prize for an essay on "The Character of Socrates," and in his senior year he again gained a prize, his subject being "The Present State of Ethical Philosophy." Among his companions he was already distinguished for literary attainments, and more especially for a certain charm in the delivery of his addresses. After graduation he entered upon his studies in the Unitarian Divinity College connected with the University. After he had graduated from the Divinity College and been "approbated" for the ministry, he was led to visit the far South—South Carolina and Florida—on account of impaired health. On his return, he was settled as the junior pastor of a large congregation in Boston, and was afterwards appointed chaplain to the State Legislature. His preaching attracted considerable attention, though it brought no crowd. Many an old hearer afterwards remembered these discourses in reading his essays. A venerable lady of those days, a member of his congregation, when asked what was his chief characteristic as a minister, said: "On God's law doth he meditate day and night."

Finding himself unable to continue to hold the creed and perform the rites of the sect with which he was connected, he decided to relinquish his pulpit. He gave his reasons for this in a remarkable discourse. The Rev. Henry Ware, whose colleague Emerson was, addressed to him a friendly expostulation against the doctrines of this discourse. In reply Emerson said: "What you say about the discourse is just what I might expect from your truth and charity, combined with your known opinions. I am not a stick or a stone, as one said in the old time, and could not feel but pain in saying some things in that place and presence which I supposed would meet with dissent, I may say, of dear friends and benefactors of mine. Yet, as my conviction is perfect in the substantial truth of the doctrines of this discourse, and is not very new, you will see at once that it must appear very important that it be spoken; and I thought I could not pay the nobleness of my friends so mean a compliment as to suppress my opposition to their supposed views, out of fear of offence. I would rather say to them—these things look thus to me, to you otherwise. Let us say our uttermost word, and let the all-pervading truth, as it surely will, judge between us. Either of us would, I doubt not, be willingly apprised of his error. Meanwhile, I shall be admonished by this experience of your thought to revise with great care the address before it is printed, and I heartily thank you for this expression of your tried toleration and love." This was followed by a sermon against Emerson's views, a copy of which was sent to him, with a letter, to which he replied. A few sentences may be given from the reply. "There is no scholar less willing or less able than myself to be a polemic. I could not give an account of myself, if challenged. I could not possibly give you one of the arguments you cruelly hint at, on which any doctrine of mine stands. For I do not know what arguments are in reference to any expression of a thought. I delight in telling what I think; but if you ask me why I dare say so, or why it is so, I am the most helpless of mortal men. When I see myself suddenly raised to the importance of a heretic, I am very uneasy when I advert to the supposed duties of such a personage, who is to make good his thesis against all comers. I certainly shall do no such thing. I shall read what you and other good men write, as I have always done, glad when you speak my thoughts, and skipping the page that has nothing for me. I shall go on just as before, seeing whatever I can, and telling what I see." This was the date of his emancipation from the trammels of creed. Shaking off all traditions of creed and authority, he stepped, as he said, into the free and open world to utter his private thought to all who were willing to hear it. Thenceforth he became "the chartered libertine" of thought, as he sometimes humorously called himself.

Emerson's earliest appearance in print, we believe, was in an address, "The Right Hand of Fellowship," delivered at the ordination of H. B. Goodwin (1830), and his next, "Sermon and Letter" to the Second Church, Boston (1832). He finally bade farewell to his Boston parish in December, 1832, and early in 1833 embarked on his first voyage to Europe. He sailed up the Mediterranean in a vessel bound for Sicily, and went as far eastward as Malta. Returning through Italy, where he dined with Walter Savage Landor in Florence—finding him "noble and courteous, living in a cloud of pictures at his villa Gherardesca"—he visited France, and in July reached London. There he saw Wellington in Westminster Abbey at the funeral of Wilberforce, and called on Coleridge. In August of the same year (1833) he made a pilgrimage to Scotland. He remained some days in Edinburgh, and delivered a discourse in the Unitarian Chapel there, recollections of which happily still survive. Desirous of personally acknowledging to Carlyle his indebtedness for the spiritual benefit he had derived from certain of his writings—notably the concluding passage in the article on German Literature, and the paper entitled "Characteristics"—he found his way, after many hindrances, to Craigenputtock, among the desolate hills of the parish of Dunscore, in Dumfriesshire, where Carlyle was then living with his bright and accomplished wife in perfect solitude, without a person to speak to, or a post office within seven miles. There he spent twenty-four hours, and became acquainted with him at once. They walked over miles of barren hills, and talked upon all the great questions which interested them most. The meeting is described in his "English Traits," published twenty-three years afterwards, and the account of it there given is reprinted by Mr. Froude in his "Life of Carlyle," &c., lately issued. Carlyle and his wife ever afterwards spoke of that visit as if it had been the coming of an angel. They regarded Emerson as a "beautiful apparition" in their solitude. A letter exists, written to a friend a few days after this visit, which gives an account of it, as well as of one to Wordsworth. This letter, written on the spur of the moment, and not intended for publication, contains some details not to be found in the published account of these two visits. It is now printed for the first time in the Appendix to this Memoir. Mr. Froude says of this visit: " The fact itself of a young American having been so affected by his writings as to have sought him out on the Dunscore moors, was a homage of the kind which he (Carlyle) could especially value and appreciate. The acquaintance then begun to their mutual pleasure ripened into a deep friendship, which has remained unclouded in spite of wide divergencies of opinion throughout their working lives, and continues warm as ever at the moment when I am writing these words (June 27, 1880), when the labours of both of them are over, and they wait in age and infirmity to be called away from a world to which they have given freely all that they had to give."

Emerson has the distinction of having been the first eminent literary man of either continent to appreciate and welcome " Sartor Resartus." The book was written in 1831 at Craigenputtock, but could find no publisher for two years. At last it appeared in " Fraser's Magazine " in successive chapters, in 1833-4 (Carlyle having to accept reduced remuneration); and it was not till 1838 that it appeared as a volume in England. While subscribers were complaining of the "intolerable balderdash " appearing from month to month in the magazine under the title of " Sartor Resartus," and threatening to withdraw their subscriptions if that "nonsense" did not speedily cease, Emerson was quietly collecting the successive numbers with a view to its publication on completion. In 1836 the American edition of the work appeared in Boston, printed, we believe, at Emerson's risk. The publication was sufficiently successful to yield a profit of £150, which Emerson sent to Carlyle—the most important sum which he had, up to that time, received for any of his works. In Emerson's modest preface to the book (on its first appearance in the shape of a volume), occur these memorable words—the earliest cordial recognition of the originality and power of this now famous work :—

> We believe, no book has been published for many years, written in a more sincere style of idiomatic English, or which discovers an equal mastery over all the riches of the language. The author makes ample amends for the occasional eccentricity of his genius, not only by frequent bursts of pure splendour, but by the wit and sense which never fail him. But what will chiefly commend the book to the discerning reader is the manifest design of the work, which is a Criticism upon the Spirit of the Age,—we had almost said, of the hour, in which we live; exhibiting, in the most just and novel light, the present aspects of Religion, Politics, Literature, Arts, and Social Life. Under all his gaiety, the writer has an earnest meaning, and discovers an insight into the manifold wants and tendencies of human nature, which is very rare among our popular authors. The philanthropy and the purity of moral sentiment, which inspire the work, will find their way to the heart of every lover of virtue.

A similar service was done by Emerson some years later in a few prefatory remarks to the first American reprint of Carlyle's Miscellaneous Reviews and Essays.

His health, which had always been delicate, and which in 1832 had been greatly affected by domestic bereavement (the death of his first wife) and the worry of controversy, was quite restored by the voyage and his subsequent travels. After his return to America he gave lectures before the Boston Lyceum, —his subjects being: "Water;" "Michael Angelo;" "Milton;" "Luther;" "George Fox;" "Edmund Burke;" also two lectures on "Italy," and three on "The Relation of Man to the Globe." In August, 1835, in a lecture before the American Institute of Instruction, his subject was the "Means of Inspiring a Taste for English Literature." In September of the same year he gave a historical address in Concord, it being the second centennial anniversary of the incorporation of that town. In September, 1835, he married Miss Lydia Jackson, of Plymouth. Her family was descended from one of the earliest Plymouth settlers. In December, 1835, he gave a course of ten lectures in Boston on "English Literature." The first two were on the earlier writers, and there were others on Chaucer, Bacon, Shakespeare, and all the subsequent great writers. In the last lecture, he touched upon Byron, Scott, Dugald Stewart, Mackintosh, and Coleridge. He placed Coleridge among the sages of the world. In succeeding seasons he gave courses on "The Philosophy of History;" "Human Culture;" "Human Life;" "The Present Age;" "The Times;" and other subjects. It is to be hoped that all these lectures, hitherto unprinted, will be given to the world. At a meeting held in Concord in 1836, on the completion of a monument to commemorate the Concord fight, a hymn was written for the occasion by Emerson, and read by Dr. Ripley, and sung to the tune of the "Old Hundred." It contained the immortal lines :—

> Here once the embattled farmers stood,
> And fired the shot heard round the world.

In 1835 he was reading Plato and Plutarch more diligently than ever, and began to study Plotinus and other writers of the same class. He also read the writings of the German mystics, as well as of the English idealists, the poems of George Herbert (which he keenly relished), and the prose works of Ralph Cudworth, Henry More, Milton, Jeremy Taylor, and Coleridge. In 1836 appeared "Nature," a little volume of only ninety-five pages, the contents consisting of an Introduction, and eight chapters, entitled, Nature, Commodity, Beauty, Language, Discipline, Idealism, Spirit, and Prospects. The spirit of its teachings is that nature exists only for the unfolding of a spiritual being. His ideas are in this little volume more systematically developed than elsewhere. They have been thus summarised :—"Every natural fact is a symbol of some spiritual fact. Nature becomes a means of expression for these spiritual truths and experiences, which could not otherwise be interpreted. Its laws, also, are moral laws when applicable to man; and so they become to man the language of the Divine Will. Because the physical laws become moral laws the moment they are related to human conduct, Nature has a much higher purpose than that of beauty or language—in that it is a Discipline. It is in these views that Emerson's resemblance to Swedenborg is apparent, in his caring for Nature only as a symbol and revelation of spiritual realities." This truly seminal book met with but a small sale,—only 500 copies being disposed of in twelve years! The first edition of it is now one of the rarest books in America. An account of the work is given by George Willis Cooke in his recent work, "Ralph Waldo Emerson: His Life, Writings, and Philosophy," to which the reader is referred. An oration, entitled "Man Thinking," delivered before the Phi-Beta-Kappa Society, Cambridge, in 1837, and an address to the Senior Divinity Class, Cambridge, 1838, also won him wide notice for their originality, boldness, and power. They exercised an immense influence on the youthful mind of New England. It was of this address that a friend of Emerson's said:—"Henceforth the young men of New England will have a fifth Gospel in their New Testaments." He delivered "Literary Ethics," an oration, in 1838.

In 1840 he started "The Dial," a magazine devoted to the discussion of mooted questions in philosophy, literature, and history. At one period of its existence Margaret Fuller and George Ripley were connected with its management. Through this organ Emerson, Ripley, Theodore Parker, Henry D. Thoreau (the most unique of American literary personalities), J. S. Dwight, W. H. Channing, Miss Fuller, C. P. Cranch, J. F. Clarke, T. H. Hedge, J. R. Lowell, Miss Peabody, A. B. Alcott, Ellery Channing, Edward, and Charles Chauncey Emerson, C. Lane, C. A. Dana, J. C. Cabot, and others,—all of them persons of high and varied culture,—gave utterance to their thoughts. The magazine existed for four years—1841-4. A complete set of the four volumes is now an almost unattainable rarity. Even odd numbers of it fetch a high price. An originally subscribed-for and complete copy exists in the library of one of Mr. Emerson's English friends, in which the authorship of each article is indicated in his own handwriting. In "The Dial" were published "Man the Reformer," "English Reformers," "The Young American," "Lectures on the Times" (including "The Conservative," and "The Transcendentalist"), "The Senses and The Soul," "Thoughts on Modern Literature," "Thoughts on Art," "The Tragic," "The Comic," "Prayers," "Letter to the Readers of 'The Dial'" (on Railroads, Air-Roads, Communities, Culture, The Position of Young Men, Bettina von Arnim, and Theodore Mandt's Account of Holderlin's "Hyperion"). Under the heading "Ethnical Scriptures" were given from time to time extracts from the most notable Oriental books of religion and morals. The first number of "The Dial" had a very characteristic address to its readers from his pen. The purpose of the magazine was—the most various expression of the best, the most cultivated, and the freest thought of the time,—and was addressed to those only who were able to find "entertainment" in such literature. There were no facts for popularity. Each number was a symposium of the most accomplished minds in the country. It is the memorial of an intellectual impulse which the national life of America has never lost. Emerson himself, in the preface to the first American edition of Carlyle's collected essays, says: "Many readers will here find pages which, in the scattered anonymous sheets of 'The Dial,' spoke to their youthful mind with an emphasis that hindered them from sleep." Many of his finest poems made their first appearance in this periodical. "The Method of Nature" was published in 1841. The first series of Emerson's "Essays," to which Mr. Carlyle contributed a preface, was published in 1841. In this volume are contained some of his most original and ablest papers—"Self-Reliance," "Compensation," "Spiritual Laws," "Love," "Friendship," "The Over-Soul," and "Intellect." In the same year he delivered an address at Concord, on the anniversary of the emancipation of the negroes in the West Indies. A second series of "Essays" appeared in 1844, also with a few prefatory words by Carlyle.

This series contained nine papers—"The Poet," "Experience," "Character," "Manners," "Gifts," "Nature," "Politics," "Nominalist and Realist," and "New England Reformers" (a lecture). In December, 1847, he wrote the "Editor's Address" in the first number of the "Massachusetts Quarterly Review."

The publication of his two volumes of Essays, having stamped Emerson as a thinker of indisputable originality and power, his fame rapidly increased in this country, and many of his admirers became desirous that he should visit England, and deliver courses of lectures, as he had done in the great towns of his own land. He had now gained the ear of England, and many of the finest minds of both hemispheres had acknowledged his genius and power. For some time he hesitated, doubting whether his name would bring together any numerous company of hearers. Several letters passed on the subject. At length his hesitancy was overcome, and permission granted by him to announce his visit and his intention to read lectures to institutions, or to any gathering of friendly individuals who sympathised with his studies. Applications immediately flowed in from every part of the kingdom, and in many cases it was found impossible to comply with the wishes of the requisitionists, from a fear of enforcing too much labour on the lecturer. Had every offer that was made been accepted, his engagements would have extended over a much longer period than he was prepared to remain in England. At last he arrived at Liverpool on 22nd October, 1847. Carlyle was greatly delighted with the prospect of again seeing his friendly visitor—"the lonely, wayfaring man," as he described him—of 1833. A letter from Emerson, announcing the probable time of his sailing, had, by negligence at a country post-office, failed to be delivered to Carlyle in due course, and only turned up near the time of Emerson's expected arrival, thus depriving the former of the opportunity of responding with hospitable messages and invitations. This led to great trouble of mind in Carlyle, fearing, as he did, that it might subject him to the appearance of a want of hospitality—a possibility abhorrent to his feelings. His trouble was ended, however, by an arrangement being made to have his reply delivered to Emerson the instant he landed in England, which, it is needless to say, was faithfully carried out. His minute instructions and almost solemn injunctions in regard to this matter were delightfully characteristic of his high regard for Emerson. The reader will find them in a later page.

For some months he took up his residence in Manchester, from which, as from a centre, he issued forth to lecture in various towns in the midland and northern counties of England. His first course was delivered to the members of the Manchester Athenæum, the subject being " Representative Men, including Plato, Swedenborg, Montaigne, Shakespeare, and Goethe." His next course was given in the Manchester Mechanics' Institution, the subjects being "Eloquence," "Domestic Life," "Reading," "The Superlative in Manners and Literature," and "The Humanity of Science." The titles of these lectures are given to show the wide range of his subjects. They excited great interest, and attracted crowded audiences. While in Manchester he delivered a remarkable speech at a soirée, held under the auspices of the Manchester Athenæum, Sir A. Alison being in the chair. Richard Cobden and other notabilities were present. His text was the indomitable "pluck" and steadfastness and grandeur of England, amid all her difficulties and trials. At that time English commerce and industry were in a very depressed condition. This speech, although comparatively brief, was carefully prepared for the occasion, and the importance he attached to it may be gathered from the fact that he printed it, *in extenso*, in his " English Traits," published nine years after. He also visited Edinburgh in February, 1848, where he lectured, and met many of its celebrities, including Robert Chambers, with whose geniality and kindly humour, and charming family circle, he was delighted. While there, he was the guest of Dr.

Samuel Brown. He spent two days at Ambleside with Miss Martineau and paid another visit to Wordsworth—his first having been paid fifteen years before. A few records of his stay in London, and remarks on some of the people he met there, will be found in his "English Traits," one of the most brilliant and striking books ever written about England and its characteristics. In perusing this volume the reader will be charmed by its vigour, vivacity, and acuteness. It is remarkable for its subtle discrimination, and clear insight into national character. In hanging over its pages, one experiences much the same feelings as if one were transplanted from a dead-level country to hilly pastures and wooded ridges, where the turf is elastic, and the air sharp, keen, and bracing.

His lectures in London were attended by the *élite* of the social and literary world of the metropolis. Mr. and Mrs. Carlyle, the Duchess of Sutherland, Lady Byron and her daughter Ada (Lady Lovelace), the Duke of Argyll, Dr. John Carlyle, William and Mary Howitt, Douglas Jerrold, Mr. John Forster, Thackeray, and many other distinguished persons were among his hearers. The writer of this notice can speak for the breathless attention of his audience, and the evident all-absorbing interest with which his discourses were listened to. The course consisted of six lectures, on "The Minds and Manners of the Nineteenth Century," "Power and Laws of Thought," "Relation of Intellect to Natural Science," "Tendencies and Duties of Men of Thought," "Politics and Socialism," "Poetry and Eloquence," and "Natural Aristocracy." It was a remarkable course. Only one or two of these lectures have been printed. Not a few of his aristocratic audience must have winced under some of his keen reproofs and reminders of duty. He uttered his convictions with a daring independence, and gave his judgments with a decisiveness of tone and earnest solemnity of manner which might have put kings in fear. He made his audience feel as if he had got them well in hand, and did not mean to let them go without giving them his "mind." It was as if he had said (to use his own words, but on another occasion):—"This you must accept as fated, and final for your salvation. It is mankind's Bill of Rights, the royal proclamation of Intellect, descending the throne, and announcing its good pleasure, that, hereafter, as *heretofore*, and now once for all, this world shall be governed by common sense and law of morals, or shall go to ruin." During the delivery of this course a letter appeared in the *London Examiner*, urging a repetition of it at a price sufficiently low to admit of poor literary men hearing Emerson. "This might be done by fixing some small admission charge, commensurate with the means of poets, critics, philosophers, historians, scholars, and the other divine paupers of that class. I feel that it ought to be done, because Emerson is a phenomenon whose like is not in the world, and to miss him is to lose an important, informing fact, out of the nineteenth century. If, therefore, you will insert this, the favour will at all events have been asked, and one conscience satisfied. It seems also probable that a very large attendance of thoughtful men would be secured, and that Emerson's stirrup-cup would be a cheering and full one, sweet and ruddy with international charity."

Three lectures were also given at Exeter Hall: "Napoleon," "Shakespeare," and "Domestic Life." At their conclusion Mr. Monckton Milnes (now Lord Houghton) made a speech complimentary to the lecturer, and to which the latter replied.

The first impression one had in listening to him in public was that his manner was so singularly quiet and unimpassioned that you began to fear the beauty and force of his thoughts were about to be marred by what might almost be described as monotony of expression. But very soon was this apprehension dispelled. The mingled dignity, sweetness, and strength of his features, the earnestness of his manner and voice, and the evident depth and sincerity of his convictions gradually extorted your deepest attention, and made you feel that you were within the grip of no ordinary man, but of one "sprung of earth's first blood," with "titles manifold;" and as he went on with serene self-possession and an air of conscious power, reading sentence after sentence, charged with well-weighed meaning, and set in words of faultless aptitude, you could no longer withstand his "so potent spell," but were forthwith compelled to surrender yourself to the fascination of his eloquence. He used little or no action, save occasionally a slight vibration of the body, as though rocking beneath the hand of some unseen power. The precious words dropped from his mouth in quick succession, and noiselessly sank into the hearts of his hearers, there to abide for ever, and, like the famed carbuncle in Eastern cave, shed a mild radiance on all things therein. Perhaps no orator ever succeeded with so little exertion in entrancing his audience, stealing away each faculty, and leading the listeners captive at his will. He abjured all force and excitement—dispensing his regal sentences in all mildness, goodness, and truth; but stealthily and surely he grew upon you, from diminutive proportions, as it were; steadily increasing, until he became a Titan, a commanding power—

> To whom, as to the mountains and the stars,
> The soul seems passive and submiss.

The moment he finished, he took up his MS. and quietly glided away,—disappearing before his audience could give vent to their applause.

The French Revolution of 1848 happening while he was in this country, he went over to Paris in the spring of that year, and was present at several meetings of the political clubs, which were then in a state of fullest activity. He was accompanied by Mr. W. E. Forster (the late Chief Secretary for Ireland). In Paris he made the acquaintance of the late James Oswald Murray, with whom he often went about the city. Mr. Murray, then an artist, made a crayon sketch of Emerson, which is in the possession of an English friend. His observations made during that visit were embodied in a brilliant lecture on the French, which he delivered at Concord, but which has not been published. Before sailing for America, in the Summer of 1848, he spent a night in Manchester, and had much to say of all he had seen and met. He overflowed with pleasant recollections of his visit, and spoke in the warmest terms of the kindness and consideration which he had everywhere experienced. He said he had not been aware there was so much kindness in the world. Would that some unseen but swift pen could have recorded all he said in these last rapidly-flying hours! Speaking of Carlyle, he repeated the words used in a letter written some months before: "The guiding genius of the man, and what constitutes his superiority over almost every other man of letters, is his commanding sense of justice, and incessant demand for sincerity." He spoke of De Quincey and Leigh Hunt as having the finest manners of any literary men he had ever met.

On the Sunday before he sailed for America, a large number of his friends and admirers from all parts of the country were invited to meet him at the hospitable mansion of Mr. and Mrs. Paulet (both since dead), near Liverpool, whose guest he was. Among other notable persons gathered together on that occasion to spend a few hours in his company, and to listen to his rich experiences and recollections, was Arthur Hugh Clough, for whom Emerson had a most tender regard. In the following year the former met Margaret Fuller in Rome. He had become known to a select circle of scholars by his poem, "The Bothie of Toper-Na-Fuosich," which Kingsley eulogised, and Oxford pronounced "indecent, immoral, profane, and communistic." Mr. Emerson esteemed the poem highly, and was the means of procuring its republication in America. In a private letter, dated December 8th, 1862, he says: "I grieve that the good Clough, the generous and susceptible scholar, should die. I have read over his 'Bothie' again, so full of the wine of youth." In the autumn of 1852 Clough went to America, by Emerson's invitation, voyaging thither in company with Thackeray and Lowell. He settled at Cambridge, Massachusetts, where he was welcomed with remarkable cordiality, and formed many friendships which lasted to the end of his life. While in America he contributed several articles to the reviews and magazines, and undertook a revision of the translation, known as Dryden's, of Plutarch's "Lives" for an American publisher, which appeared in five volumes. In the following year he returned to England. He died at Florence in 1861, in his 43rd year.

In 1846 Emerson published his first volume of Poems; in 1850 the "Essay on War" in Miss Peabody's "Aesthetic Papers;" and "Representative Men;" and in 1852, in conjunction with W. H. Channing, the "Memoirs of Margaret Fuller." His contribution to the work were the chapters in the first volume on Concord and Boston. Four years later (1856), he published "English Traits." Under the title of "Echoes of Harper's Ferry" he published, in 1860, three speeches concerning John Brown, which he had delivered at Boston in 1859, at Concord later in the same year, and at Salem in 1860. This was followed by "The Conduct of Life" (1860), containing nine essays—Fate, Power, Wealth, Culture, Behaviour, Worship, Considerations by the Way, Beauty, Illusions. In 1864 appeared an "Introductory Essay on Persian Poetry," prefixed to the "Gulistan" of Saadi; Biographical Sketch prefixed to H. D. Thoreau's "Excursions" (1863), "Oration on the Death of President Lincoln" (1865), "May-day and other Poems" (1867), "Address at a Meeting to organize the Free Religious Association" (1867); "The Rule of Life," a Lecture delivered to the "Parker Fraternity" (1867); "Society and Solitude" (1870), containing twelve essays—Society and Solitude, Civilization, Art, Eloquence, Domestic Life, Farming, Work and Days, Books, Clubs, Courage, Success, Old Age. In 1871 he wrote an introduction to Goodwin's translation of Plutarch's "Morals."

In the same year appeared "Parnassus, a Selection of English and American Poetry, with prefatory remarks," of which it may be truly said that it is the best collection of English Poetry ever made. The only thing marring the completeness of the volume is the much-to-be-regretted absence of a few specimens of his own poems. Any other selector but Emerson would—had he been a poet—have given some specimens of his own verses. In a recent volume of "Selections of English Poetry," published in London, the editor obligingly presents the reader with eleven passages from Shakespeare, seven from Milton, and *thirteen* from his own works! Some of the selections in "Parnassus" have been inserted for their "historical importance; some for their weight of sense; some for single couplets or lines, perhaps even for a word; some for magic of style; and others which—although in their structure betraying a defect of poetic ear—have nevertheless a wealth of truth which ought to have created melody." The arrangement is not chronological, but based upon the character of the subject, under the following heads: Nature; Human Life; Intellectual; Contemplative, Moral and Religious; Heroic; Portraits; Narrative Poems and Ballads; Songs; Dirges and Pathetic Poems; Comic and Humorous; Poetry of Terror, and Oracles and Counsels. An index of authors, prefixed, with dates of birth and death, is a useful guide in many instances, especially as regards the period of the writings. It does not appear that the merits of the author's acknowledged—or perhaps we should say recognised—position had had much to do with the copiousness of the extracts. The next products of his pen were an Address on "The Dedication of the Concord Free Library" (1873); and in 1876 "Letters and Social Aims," containing eleven essays—Poetry and Imagination, Social Aims, Eloquence, Resources, The Comic, Quotation and Originality, Progress of Culture, Persian Poetry, Inspiration, Greatness,

Immortality; "Fortune of the Republic," an address delivered in Boston in February, 1878; and "The Preacher," printed in the "Unitarian Review" (1880). In the "North American Review" will be found the following essays:—Michael Angelo, Milton, Character, Demonology, Perpetual Forces, The Sovereignty of Ethics. To the "Atlantic Monthly" he contributed, between 1858 and 1876, the following articles and poems:—The Rommany Girl, The Chartist's Complaint, Days, Brahma, Illusions, Solitude and Society, Two Rivers, Books, Persian Poetry, Eloquence, Waldeinsamkeit, Song of Nature, Culture, The Test, Old Age, The Titmouse, American Civilization, Compensation, Thoreau, The President's Proclamation, Boston Hymn, Voluntaries, Saadi, My Garden, Boston, Terminus, Aspects of Culture (Phi-Beta-Kappa Address, Harv. Univ., 1867).

In a later page the reader will find a list of the articles on Emerson and his writings in the magazines and reviews of Great Britain and the United States, as well as indications of what has been written about him in France, Germany, and Holland.

In 1872 he again visited Europe, accompanied by his daughter, arriving in November. After a short stay in London, they proceeded to Egypt, spending some time there, returning in the Spring of 1873 to England, *via* Italy and France. During this visit he did not deliver any lectures. He resided for some weeks in London, and visited Professor Max Müller at Oxford. He spent a single day (8th May) in Edinburgh, his main object being to see Dr. J. Hutchison Stirling, author of "The Secret of Hegel." His two last days were spent under the roof of a friend in Cheshire, and many of his old acquaintances and hearers of 1847-8 had thus an opportunity of meeting him.

The friendship which existed between Emerson and that remarkable woman, Margaret Fuller—was altogether of a noble and beautiful character, and was only terminated by her sad and untimely death. Returning from Europe with her husband (Count D'Ossoli) and child, the vessel in which they sailed was wrecked on 16th June, 1850, within sight of her own New England shores—indeed, quite close to the beach. For twelve agonising hours they were face to face with death. She refused an attempt made by four of the crew to save her, lest she might have been divided for ever from those dearest to her. She bravely preferred certain death to the chances of an eternal separation. The terrible story has been told with intense power and sympathy by W. H. Channing. Of this woman of true genius, whose conversation was of unrivalled fluency and brilliancy, ample records remain. She was an accomplished Greek, Latin, and Hebrew scholar. She had a singular power of communicating her literary enthusiasm to her companions. She has left behind her several volumes containing the best of her literary work. It has been said of her that "she was plain in appearance, and that she had a faculty of unsheathing herself at the touch of a thought; and those who came into right relations with her remember her as almost beautiful. Her natural place was at the centre of a circle where thoughts and truths were being discovered, and which had not yet found their channels in literature. With the finest womanly sympathies she combined the strong masculine intellect, and an individuality which stimulated every other individuality. Her influence was great in the intellectual activities of her day." She has left a record of her impressions of Emerson's Lectures, too long for quotation in full, but from which it is worth while giving a few sentences: "Among his audience some there were—simple souls—whose life had been, perhaps, without clear light, yet still a search after truth for its own sake, who were able to recognise beneath his veil of words the still small voice of conscience, the vestal fires of lone religious hours, and the mild teachings of the summer woods. The charm of his elocution was great. His general manner was that of the reader, occasionally rising into direct address or invocation in passages where tenderness or majesty demanded more energy. At such times both eye and voice called on a remote future to give a worthy reply—a future which shall manifest more largely the universal soul as it was then manifest to his soul. The tone of the voice was a grave body tone, full and sweet rather than sonorous, yet flexible, and haunted by many modulations, as even instruments of wood and brass seem to become after they have been long played on with skill and taste; how much more so the human voice! In the most expressive passages it uttered notes of silvery clearness, winning, yet still more commanding. The words uttered in those tones floated awhile above us, then took root in the memory like winged seed. In the union of an even rustic plainness with lyric inspiration, religious dignity with philosophic calmness, keen sagacity in details with boldness of view, we saw what brought to mind the early poets and legislators of Greece—men who taught their fellows to plough and avoid moral evil, sing hymns to the gods, and watch the metamorphosis of nature. Here in civic Boston was such a man—one who could see man in his original grandeur and his original childishness, rooted in simple nature, raising to the heavens the brow and eye of a poet." An account of Concord and Emerson is given at length by Frederika Bremer, in her "Homes of the New World." She was a guest in Emerson's house, and describes her host and his environments in a most vivid manner.

Every reader of Mr. Lowell knows his intensely humorous description of the characteristics of Emerson and Carlyle, given in "A Fable for Critics." The keen and vigorous critic has said many admirable things in prose about Emerson which are well worth remembering. Here are a few of them: "A lecturer now for something like a third of a century, one of the pioneers of the lecturing system, the charm of his voice, his manner, and his matter has never lost its power over his earlier hearers, and continually winds new ones in its en-

chanting meshes." "There is no man living to whom, as a writer, so many of us feel and thankfully acknowledge so great an indebtedness for ennobling impulses. We look upon him as one of the few men of genius whom our age has produced. Search for his eloquence in his books, and you will perchance miss it, but meanwhile you will find that it has kindled all your thoughts. For choice and pith of language he belongs to a better age than ours, and might rub shoulders with Fuller and Sir Thomas Browne—a diction at once so rich and so homely as his I know not where to match. It is like homespun cloth-of-gold. I know no one that can hold a promiscuous crowd in pleased attention so long as he. . . .
'Plain living and high thinking' speak to us in this altogether unique lay-preacher. We have shared in the beneficence of this varied culture, this fearless impartiality in criticism and speculation, this masculine sincerity, this sweetness of nature which rather stimulates than cloys, for a generation long. If ever there was a standing testimonial to the cumulative power and value of Character—we have it in this gracious and dignified presence. What an antiseptic is a pure life! At sixty-five he has that privilege of soul which abolishes the calendar, and presents him to us always the unwasted contemporary of his own prime. . . . Who that saw the audience will ever forget it, where every one still capable of fire, or longing to renew in them the half-forgotten sense of it, was gathered? Those faces, young and old, agleam with pale intellectual light, eager with pleased attention, flash upon me once more from the deep recesses of the years with an exquisite pathos. Ah, beautiful young eyes, brimming with love and hope, wholly vanished now in that other world we call the Past, or peering doubtfully through the pensive gloaming of memory, your light impoverishes these cheaper days! I hear again that rustle of sensation, as they turned to exchange glances over some pithier thought, some keener flash of that humour which always played about the horizon of his mind

like heat-lightning, and it seems now like the sad whisper of the autumn leaves that are whirling around me." "His younger hearers could not know how much they owed to the benign impersonality, that quiet scorn of everything ignoble, the never-sated hunger of self-culture, that were personified in the man before them. But the older knew how much the country's intellectual emancipation was due to the stimulus of his teaching and example, how constantly he had kept burning the beacon of an ideal life above our lower region of turmoil. To him more than to all other causes did the young martyrs of our Civil War owe the sustaining strength of thoughtful heroism that is so touching in every record of their lives. Those who are grateful to Mr. Emerson, as many of us are, for what they feel to be most valuable in their culture, or perhaps I should say their impulse, are grateful not so much for any direct teachings of his as for that inspiring *lift* which only genius can give, and without which all doctrine is chaff." "I can never help applying to him what Ben Jonson said of Bacon—'There happened in my time one noble speaker, who was full of gravity in his speaking. His language was nobly censorious. No man ever spoke more neatly, more pressly, more weightily, or suffered less emptiness, less idleness, in what he uttered. No member of his speech but consisted of his own graces. His hearers could not cough, or look aside from him, without loss. He commanded where he spoke.'"

Mr. Lowell gives a vivid description of the effect produced by Emerson's speech at the Burns' Centenary dinner at Boston in 1859. "In that closely-filed speech of his every word seemed to have just dropped from the clouds. He looked far away over the heads of his hearers with a vague kind of expectation, as into some private heaven of invention, and the winged period came at last obedient to his spell. . . Every sentence brought down the house, as I never saw one brought down before,—and it is not so easy to heat Scotsmen with a sentiment that has no hint of native brogue in it. I watched, for it was an interesting study, how the quick sympathy ran flashing from face to face down the long tables, like an electric spark thrilling as it went, and then exploded in a thunder of plaudits. I watched till tables and faces vanished, for I, too, found myself caught up in the common enthusiasm." Emerson's concluding sentences were these:—

Yet how true a poet is he ! and the poet, too, of poor men, of grey hodden, and the guernsey coat, and the blouse. He has given voice to all the experiences of common life ; he has endeared the farm-house and cottage, patches and poverty, beans and barley; ale, the poor man's wine ; hardship, the fear of debt, the dear society of weans and wife, of brothers and sisters, proud of each other, knowing so few, and finding amends for want and obscurity in books and thought. What a love of nature, and, shall I say it ? of middle-class nature. Not great like Goethe in the stars, or like Byron on the ocean, or Moore in the luxurious East, but in the lonely landscape which the poor see around them, bleak leagues of pasture and stubble, ice, and sleet, and rain, and snow-choked brooks; birds, hares, field-mice, thistles and heather, which he daily knew. How many "Bonnie Doons," and "John Anderson, my joes," and "Auld Langsynes," all round the earth have his verses been applied to ! And his love songs still woo and melt the youths and maids ; the farm-work, the country holiday, the fishing coble, are still his debtors to-day. And as he was thus the poet of poor, anxious, cheerful, working humanity, so he had the language of low life. He grew up in a rural district, speaking a patois unintelligible to all but natives, and he has made that lowland Scotch a Doric dialect of fame. It is the only example in history of a language made classic by the genius of a single man. But more than this, he had that secret of genius, to draw from the bottom of society the strength of its speech, and astonish the ears of the polite with these artless words, better than art, and filtered of all offence through his beauty. It seemed odious to Luther that the devil should have all the best tunes ; he would bring them into the churches ; and Burns knew how to take from fairs and gypsies, blacksmiths and drovers, the speech of the market and street, and clothe it with melody. But I am detaining you too long. The memory of Burns—I am afraid heaven and earth have taken too good care of it, to leave us anything to say. The west winds are murmuring it. Open the windows behind you, and hearken for the incoming tide what the waves say of it. The doves perching always on the eaves of the stone chapel opposite may know something of it. Every name in broad Scotland keeps his fame bright. The memory of Burns—every man's and boy's, and girl's head carries snatches of his songs, and can say them by heart, and, what is strangest of all, never learned them from a book, but from mouth to mouth. The wind whispers them, the birds whistle them, the corn, barley, and bulrushes hoarsely rustle them ; nay, the music-boxes at Geneva are framed and toothed to play them ; the hand organs of the Savoyards in all cities repeat them, and the chimes of bells ring them in the spires. They are the property and the solace of mankind.

From an Essay on Emerson by John Burroughs, the author of several volumes of rare merit, published in New York, and which it is surprising no London publisher has yet introduced to British readers, it is worth while giving a few sentences, bearing upon some of the characteristics of Mr. Emerson's writings. Mr. Burroughs wields a racy pen, and there is the ring of the true metal in his delightful sketches of outdoor nature, mingled with chapters of a more purely literary character.

I know of no other writing that yields the reader so many strongly stamped medallion-like sayings and distinctions. There is a perpetual refining and recoining of the current wisdom of life and conversation. It is the old gold or silver or copper; but how bright and new it looks in his pages! Emerson loves facts, things, objects, as the workman his tools. He makes everything serve. The stress of expression is so great that he bends the most obdurate element to his purpose; as the bird, under her keen necessity, weaves the most contrary and diverse materials into her nest. He seems to like best material that is a little refractory; it makes his page more piquant and stimulating. Within certain limits he loves roughness, but not to the expense of harmony. He has a wonderful hardiness and push. Where else in literature is there a mind, moving in so rare a medium, that gives one such a sense of tangible resistance and force?

. . . .

But after we have made all possible deductions from Emerson there remains the fact that he is a living force, and, tried by home standards, a master. Wherein does the secret of his power lie? He is the prophet and philosopher of young men. The old man and the man of the world make little of him, but of the youth who is ripe for him he takes almost an unfair advantage. One secret of his charm I take to be the instant success with which he transfers our interest in the romantic, the chivalrous, the heroic, to the sphere of morals and the intellect. We are let into another realm unlooked for, where daring and imagination also lead. The secret and suppressed heart finds a champion. To the young man fed upon the penny precepts and staple Johnsonianism of English literature, and of what is generally doled out in the schools and colleges, it is a surprise; it is a revelation. A new world opens before him. The nebulæ of his spirit are resolved or shown to be irresolvable. The fixed stars of his inner firmament are brought immeasurably near. He drops all other books. . . . Emerson is the knight errant of the moral sentiment. He leads in our time and country, one illustrious division, at least, in the holy crusade of the affections and the intuitions against the usurpations of tradition and theological dogma.

Emerson often appeared on the Anti-Slavery platform, and sympathised warmly with the Abolitionists. His views on Free Trade were of the most far-reaching nature. "America," he said in one of his public addresses, "means opportunity, freedom, power. The genius of this country has marked out her true policy; opportunity—doors wide open—every port open. If I could I would have Free Trade with all the world, without toll or custom-house. Let us invite every nation, every race, every skin; white man, black man, red man, yellow man. Let us offer hospitality, a fair field, and equal laws to all. The land is wide enough, the soil has food enough for all. We should cling to the common school, and enlarge and extend the opportunities it offers. Let us educate every soul. Every native child, and every foreign child that is cast on our coast should be taught, at the public cost, first, the rudiments of knowledge, and then, as far as may be, the ripest results of art and science." An acute writer in the *Spectator*, of May 6th, 1882, speaking of the interest Emerson took in all public events, very justly remarks: "He sympathised ardently with all the great practical movements of his own day, while Carlyle held contemptuously aloof. He was one of the first to strike a heavy blow at the institution of slavery. He came forward to encourage his country in the good cause, when slavery raised the flag of rebellion. He had a genuine desire to see all men free, while Carlyle only felt the desire to see all men strongly governed—which they might be, without being free at all. Emerson's spirit, moreover, was much the saner, and more reverent of the two, though less rich in power and humour."

During the last three or four years his memory frequently failed him, especially in reference to his recollection of more recent events. But he was himself perfectly conscious of this, and though it did not prevent his occasionally delivering lectures and taking part in public gatherings, from the time this defect became manifest he was always accompanied to the platform by his daughter, whose devotion and considerate tact invariably supplied the words and phrases which Mr. Emerson could not recall. To the last he continued to take great interest in the well-being of his neighbours and the intellectual and material progress of his native village. He had never lost his inherent love of dignified simplicity in domestic life, and his home was a model of refinement and unostentatious comfort. He was never more happy than in the company of his grandchildren, and all children loved him. His old age was serene, and the sweetness and gentleness of his character were more and more apparent as the years rolled on. To the last, even when the events of yesterday were occasionally obscured, his memory of the remote past was unclouded. He would talk about the friends of his early and middle life with unbroken vigour; and those who ever had the good fortune to hear him, in the free intercourse of his own study, will not soon forget the charm of his conversation and the graciousness of his demeanour. He would drive with his visitors to the numerous interesting spots in and about Concord, he would point out the old home of his own family, the house of his friend, Mr. Alcott, and the still more famous "old manse" which Hawthorne has made immortal. One who had the pleasure of visiting him within the last two years has told of such a privilege; how he saw the wise old man whom he had first heard in Manchester more than thirty years before, and again in the seclusion of a friend's house during Mr. Emerson's last visit to England, and at last in the home of his youth and age. "Assuredly," he said, "this great and good man was seldom seen to rarer advantage. He drove me to the haunts of the pilgrims who came to Concord to see the place of so many noble and interesting associations; in the public library of the town which he had helped to establish, he showed me not a few literary treasures which the greatest libraries in the world might envy—he pointed out the famous tavern where the British soldiers stopped on the day made memorable by the first fight in the war of Independence. And on the battle field itself, where the beautiful Concord river still flows silently between the low hills which almost entwine the little town, he told the story of the famous struggle. It was a perfect spring day; light breezes stirred the pine trees under which lay the remains of the nameless English soldiers; and hard by was the granite monument to the memory of the local militiamen who fell in that famous skirmish. The scenes and the associations were in themselves eloquent, but they were rendered immeasurably more so by the narrative of the sage whose verses, cut in stone on the monument before us, will tell of future generations how Concord's noblest son sang of the renown of his country's defenders. And a few weeks afterwards I was present at one of the dinners of the famous Saturday Club. As the wits of the Restoration and Queen Anne's days met at Wills's Coffee House to listen to Dryden or to the more select conclave of the October Club, so the poets essayists, and humourists of Boston assembled at these dinners, held sometimes at the houses of the members, and sometimes, when the meetings were larger, in one of the hotels. This was a notable gathering; it was intended to do special honour to the distinguished Massachusetts lawyer, who had just returned from presiding at the Chicago Convention which had nominated General Garfield, Republican candidate, for the Presidency. Longfellow was in the chair; James T. Fields was near him. Dr. Oliver Wendell Holmes was as usual the life and soul of the party, and there were other scarcely less famous men. Emerson had not recently been able to attend many of the meetings, but the occasion was no ordinary one. 'Look at Emerson,' said Fields; 'how happy he looks; was there ever such a sweet smile, and yet how silent he is. In the early days of the club, when Agassiz, its founder, was with us, he and Emerson were the liveliest of us all.' It was touching to see the marks of reverence and regard which all displayed to him, and to notice his appreciatory responses. He thoroughly enjoyed the sparkling sallies of Wendell Holmes, and when

Longfellow, to whom speech-making was always a punishment, in a few well-chosen words, referred to the presence of their honoured fellow-member, Emerson was constrained to reply, and he did not forget to tell us that if he could not make them a speech he was only following the example of his friend the chairman. It was altogether a delightful meeting, but already there are melancholy associations with it. Fields, whose 'Yesterdays with Authors' has given us so many delightful sketches of famous men, has followed his friends Thackeray and Dickens. Longfellow, the sweetest, the most genial, and gentle of poets and men, has also gone, and now we mourn the departure of the greatest of them, Emerson himself, a man in whom were combined the strength of the New England Puritan and the grace and beauty of the accomplished Greek."

Did space permit, much might be said of Emerson's first visit to England in 1833, and his second in 1847-8; of the tenor of his life at Concord; of the literary contemporaries and friends who sought his society and counsel; of his connection with the notable experiment of the Brook Farm community (although he never joined it), idealised by the weird pen of Hawthorne in the "Blithedale Romance;" of his literary tours; of his imperturbable good temper, and sweetness of nature—the rare union in him of humility and nobility—producing (to use the words of a living author) "the most perfect gentleman he ever met;" of the accidental destruction of his house by fire, and his year's absence in Europe, while it was being rebuilt at the expense of his fellow-townsmen, as a mark of their regard; and of the enthusiasm with which he was received on his return — the crowd accompanying him in triumph from the railway station to the newly-built house, which, with delicate and thoughtful consideration, had been made an exact counterpart of the old home. A letter from one of his own family, written at the time, records that the citizens gathered at the railway terminus in crowds, and the school children were drawn up in two smiling rows, through which he passed, greeted by enthusiastic cheers and songs of welcome. All followed his carriage to the house, and sang "Home, sweet Home" to the music of the band. A few days afterwards, he invited all his fellow-citizens to call and see him in his new home, and most of the inhabitants availed themselves of the opportunity.

With regard to his claims as a poet, a few words only can be said. The essence of true poetry is manifest in many of his sayings that take not the form of versification. It has been truly said that the highest and best poetry is that which is felt, and which is incapable of being expressed in language. He is emphatically a poet in his prose. His poems contain genuine inspiration of the very highest kind, but rhyme does not aid his development. In a single page he gives more of the spirit of poetry than would supply a dozen of ordinary rhymesters for the whole of their lives; and yet there are poetasters who could at least equal him in the construction of passable verses. When the world is wiser, Emerson will be owned as a great poet. There are single poems of his which for depth of feeling, tender regret, profound insight into the human soul, and an inimitable quaintness and simplicity (sometimes rivalling George Herbert himself) are not to be matched in the works of the acknowledged masters of the poetic art. His friend, Dr. Hedge, says:—"In poetic art he does not excel. The verses often halt, the conclusion sometimes flags, and metrical propriety is recklessly violated. But this defect is closely connected with the characteristic merit of the poet, and springs from the same root—his utter spontaneity. And this spontaneity is but a mode of his sincerity. More than those of any of his contemporaries, his poems, for the most part, are inspirations. They are not made, but given; they come of themselves. They are not meditated, but burst from the soul with an irrepressible necessity of utterance— sometimes with a rush which defies the shaping intellect. It seems as if it were not the man himself that speaks, but a power behind—call it Daemon or Muse. Where the Muse flags, it is her fault, not his; he is not going to help her out with wilful elaboration or emendation. There is no trace, as in most poetry, of joiner-work, and no mark of the file." The following remarks relating to his poems are from the pen of an English friend—one of his most appreciative admirers—in a letter written since the news of his death:—

"I well recollect the wonder with which I first became familiar with those crystal-clear perceptions of his,—visions as if from the very mountain top of the human intellect. To me they were a distinct revelation of new intellectual possibilities, hitherto only dimly imagined. We talk, naturally enough, of Emerson being one of the greatest of American writers; to me he has always stood alone in the great history of literature—the clearest seer, the most dauntless speaker, the deftest and most subtle intellect; uttering his convictions in words of light tinted only from the azure of infinity. I know nothing more exquisitely dainty than some of his snatches of poetry. Those who see no poetry in them, simply do not see them at all. I can only compare them to exquisite snow-crystals, fresh gathered from some highest mountain peak, where the clouds of human infirmity never reach. Human passion, in the Edgar Poe sense, they have none; but for subtlety of insight and delicacy of utterance, I think they stand alone in literature."

As regards Emerson's literary methods, one of his friends thus speaks: "It was his habit to spend the forenoon in his study, with constant regularity. He did not wait for moods, but caught them as they came, and used their results in each day's work. It was his wont to jot down his thoughts at all hours and places. The suggestions resulting from his readings, conversations, and meditations, were immediately transferred to the note-book he always carried with him. In his walks, many a gem of thought was in this way preserved.

C

Even during the night he would get up and jot down some thought worth laying hold of. All the results of his thinking were thus stored up, to be made use of when required. After his note-books were filled, he transcribed their contents in a large commonplace book. When a fresh subject possessed his mind, he brought together the jottings he found he had written down concerning it, forming them into a connected whole, with additional material suggested at the time. His essays were thus very slowly elaborated, wrought out through days and months, and even years, of patient thought. They were all carefully revised, again and again; corrected, wrought over, portions dropped, new matter added, or the paragraphs arranged in a new order. He was unsparing in his corrections, striking out sentence after sentence; and whole paragraphs disappear from time to time. His manuscript was everywhere filled with erasures and emendations; scarcely a page that was not covered with these evidences of his diligent revision."

A friend says that few authors have published less than Emerson in comparison with the great mass of papers which remain unprinted. "Scarcely any of his numerous sermons have ever been published; most of his speeches on political and social occasions remain uncollected and unedited; many verses exist only in manuscript, or have been withdrawn from publication; and even of his lectures, from which he has printed freely for nearly forty years, a great many still remain in manuscript. Even those published omit much that was spoken,—the five lectures on History, on Love, and others, displaying so many omissions to those who heard them, that the author was at the time sorely complained of by his faithful hearers for leaving out so much that had delighted them. Few or none of the philosophical lectures read at Harvard University eight or nine years ago, and designed to make part of what he called 'The Natural History of the Intellect,' have ever been printed. This work, when completed, was to be the author's most systematic and connected treatise. It was to contain, what could not fail to be of interest to all readers, his observations on his own intellectual processes and methods, of which he has always been studiously watchful, and which, from his habit of writing, he has carefully noted down. From this work, which, even if not finished, will at some time be printed, and from his correspondence of these many years, portions of which will finally be printed, it will be possible to reconstruct hereafter a rare and remarkable episode in literary history."

An American writer, speaking of Emerson's unwillingness to print anything but his best, says :—" He has always been extremely careful of what he put into print, regarding the covers of a book as a sacred temple into which only the purest and best of a writer should be permitted to enter. No American or European has been so superlatively fastidious as he respecting publication. He believed that a book should have every reason for being ; that nothing trivial, passing, or temporary should be introduced into it ; that the sole excuse for a book should be the presentation of fresh thought ; that its contents should be in some manner an addition to the common stock of knowledge. Most authors would have put all their lectures and essays between covers because they had written them, and because they could gain something thereby. Emerson was an illustrious example to his guild in this particular. If he had less vanity than members of his craft generally he had more pride, more regard for his reputation, more confident expectation of enduring fame. It is said that he had unwavering confidence in this, and that therefore he published what was universal and abiding in interest and influence, and compressed his utterances into the smallest space. Had all writers followed his example how immeasurably libraries would have been reduced ! A hundred volumes would shrink to one, and there might be some hope of a tireless student in a long life gaining a slight smattering of the great authors with whom everybody is presumed to be wholly familiar. Emerson is a pattern to all mere book-makers present and to come. If he had done nothing else than to inculcate by example the economy of print he would deserve a separate niche in the temple of literary fame, and who shall say that he has not secured it? All the writings he has wished to be known by can be put into three small volumes, and in these is there not as much weighty and important matter as can be discovered in the same space in any language? The matter is not (as in the great majority of books) what can be found elsewhere—generally far better said—in the illimitable wilderness of type. It is, barring quotations, which always serve to illustrate his idea, actually Emerson's own, the fruit of his observation, study, and reflection—the action of an original individual mind upon life, history, and nature."

Professor Tyndall thus speaks of his reason for so often quoting Emerson:—" I do so mainly because in him we have a poet and a profoundly religious man, who is really and entirely undaunted by the discoveries of science—past, present, or prospective. In his case poetry, with the joy of a bacchanal, takes her graver brother science by the hand and cheers him with immortal laughter. By Emerson scientific conceptions are continually transmuted into the finer forms and warmer hues of an ideal world." "If anyone can be said to have given the impulse to my mind, it is Emerson; whatever I have done, the world owes to him." It is said that on the fly-leaf of an odd volume of Emerson's works, accidentally picked up by the Professor at an old-book stall, and which first made him acquainted with his writings, are inscribed these words: " Purchased by inspiration." Herman Grimm, an accomplished German critic of Emerson, says that he found in his works a sense of joy and beauty, such as is given by the greatest books. He found himself made captive by thoughts which it seemed as if he were hearing for the first time. "When I again read his sentences," he continues, "the enchanting breezes of hope and spiritual joy filled my soul anew. The old worn-out machinery of the world was re-created, and I felt as if I had never breathed so heavenly an atmosphere. I can indeed say that no author has had such an influence upon me as Emerson. The manner of writing of the man, whom I hold to be the greatest of all living authors, has revealed to me a new way of expressing thought." The late Dean Stanley concludes a letter about him in these words:—" Long may Ralph Waldo Emerson enjoy the influence which superiority gives over mediocrity, and calm reason over fleeting passion."

Whatever verdict may be pronounced upon Emerson's opinions, he must be universally regarded as one who by his teaching and practical example has done more to make the life of the scholar beautiful, and the career of the man of letters a reproof to all low aims, and an inspiration to all high ones, than any other man in America—one might almost say, in either continent. His greatest service has been the inculcation of intellectual self-reliance, and absolute sincerity of thought. In an oration delivered before the literary societies of Dartmouth College in July, 1838, will be found the highest expression of his opinion regarding the duty and aims of the scholar :—

If, with a high trust, he can thus submit himself to the supreme soul, he will find that ample returns are poured into his bosom, out of what seemed hours of obstruction and loss. Let him not grieve too much on account of unfit associates. When he sees how much thought he owes to the disagreeable antagonism of various persons who pass and cross him, he can easily think that in a society of perfect sympathy, no word, no act, no record, would be. He will learn that it is not much matter what he reads, what he does. Be a scholar, and he shall have the scholar's part of everything. As, in the counting room, the merchant cares little whether the cargo be hides or barilla ; the transaction, a letter of credit or a transfer of stocks ; be it what it may, his commission comes gently out of it ; so you shall get your lesson out of the hour, and the object, whether it be a concentrated or a wasteful employment, even in reading a dull book, or working off a stint of mechanical day labour, which your necessities or the necessities of others impose. . . .

Be content with a little light, so it be your own. Explore, and explore, and explore. Be neither chided nor flattered out of your position of perpetual inquiry.

Neither dogmatize yourself, nor accept another's dogmatism. Why should you renounce your right to traverse the star-lit deserts of truth, for the premature comforts of an acre, house, or barn? Truth also has its roof, and bed, and board. Make yourself necessary to the world, and mankind will give you bread, and if not store of it, yet such as shall not take away your property in all men's possessions, in all men's affections, in art, in nature, and in hope. You will not fear that I am enjoining too stern an asceticism. Ask not, Of what use is a scholarship that systematically retreats? or Who is the better for the philosopher who conceals his accomplishments, and hides his thoughts from the waiting world? Hides his thoughts! Hide the sun and moon. Thought is all light, and publishes itself to the universe. It will speak, though you were dumb, by its own miraculous organ. It will flow out of your actions, your manners, and your face. It will bring you friendships. It will impledge you to truth by the love and expectation of generous minds. By virtue of the laws of that Nature, which is one and perfect, it will yield every sincere good that is in the soul, to the scholar beloved of earth and heaven.

Emerson is also one of the consummate masters of the English tongue. "His sentences are often like diamonds. There is no thinker of our day who, for sentences that have the ring of oracles, can quite compare with him." "No writer is so quotable. Scarcely a page, especially of the earlier essays, but supplies some terse and pregnant saying, worthy to be inscribed in a golden treasury of portable wisdom." "His sentences score themselves on the brain. Force of statement, the surprise of fitness, the hitting of the nail on the head—are the distinguishing characteristics of his writings." "His pages are laden with aphorisms—his style of composition is eminently aphoristic—and they are so felicitously put, and on such a variety of themes, that the capturing memory declines to surrender them, and speedily claims them as its own. Let him the fit audience find, though few, and he will illustrate what it is to speak golden words in that natural style of perfect sincerity, tenderness, and thoughtfulness, by which every syllable is conducted straight home to the faculty it was meant for. For the enunciation of his own sentences we call him simply a perfect speaker. The manner fits the matter as if cut out for it from eternity."

Theodore Parker, in one of the best critical papers on Emerson that has appeared, written in 1849, says: "He is the most republican of republicans, the most protestant of dissenters. His culture is cosmopolitan. He trusts himself, trusts man, and trusts God. He has confidence in all the attributes of Infinity. Hence he is serene; nothing disturbs the even poise of his character, and he walks erect. Nothing impedes him in his search for the true, the lovely, and the good; no private hope, no private fear, no love of wife or child or gold or ease or fame. He has not written a line which is not conceived in the interest of mankind. He never writes in the interest of a section, of a party, of a church, of a man, but always in the interest of mankind. No faithful man is too low for his approval and encouragement; no faithless man too high and popular for his rebuke. To no English writer, since Milton, can be assigned so high a place; even Milton himself, great genius though he was, and great architect of beauty, has not added so many thoughts to the treasury of the race; no, nor been the author of so much loveliness. Emerson is a man of genius such as does not often appear; such as has never appeared before in America, and but seldom in the world. He learns from all sorts of men; but no English writer, we think, is so original."

In a brief memoir like this, it would be out of place to attempt to explain his philosophy. He has, in fact, propounded no system. He is called a Transcendentalist; but he never adopted the name. He beholds and reports all, be it secular or sacred. "He trustingly accepts what comes to the open sense and the waiting mind." "Strictly, he is not the founder of any school, but has furnished the foundation stones of many schools." "If he has not discovered the secret of the universe, he tells frankly what he finds as a perceiver or observer, and constantly endeavours to place himself in harmony with the Most High." He seeks to solve the riddle of the universe for himself, and is content with no traditionary answer. He insists on man's individuality, and protests against the merging of our separate beings into indolent conformity with a majority. "Let a man know his worth, and keep things under his feet. Beneath opinions, habits, customs, is the spirit of a man. The one thing in the world of value is the soul,—free, sovereign, active. He teaches that man shall be true to himself, let the world say what it will. The truly religious mind will find beauty and necessary facts,—in the shop and the mill. Proceeding from a religious heart, it will raise to a divine use the railroad, the insurance office, the telegraph, the chemist's retort,—in which we now seek only an economic use. The end and aim of life is not to assert ourselves, but by individual faithfulness to become fit recipients of the Divine Mind, so as to live in thoughts and act with energies which are immortal. The greatest philosopher is but the listener of simple faithfulness; and the loftiest wisdom is gained when self is forgotten in communion with God." To use his own words, "Let man thus learn the revelation of all nature and all thought to his heart; this, namely, that the Highest dwelleth with him; that the sources of Nature are in his own mind, if the sentiment of duty be there." "Let it not be recorded, that in this moment of the Eternity, when we who were named by our names, flitted across the light, we were afraid of any fact, or disgraced the fair day by a pusillanimous preference of our bread to our freedom. What is the scholar, what is the man *for*, but for hospitality to every new thought of his time? Have you leisure, power, property, friends? you shall be the asylum and patron of every new thought, every unproven opinion, every untried project, which proceeds out of goodwill and honest seeking. All the newspapers, all the tongues of to-day will of course at first defame what is noble; but you who hold not of to-day, not of the times, but of the Everlasting, are to stand for it; and the highest compliment Man ever receives from Heaven, is the sending to him its disguised and discredited angels."

Those who have felt throughout their lives the purifying and elevating power of Emerson's writings, and who have recognised in his inspiring career the perfect sanity of true genius, can never think of him without affectionate reverence. He now rests, in that deep repose which he has so well earned, and on laurels that will never fade.

FUNERAL.

The Funeral of Ralph Waldo Emerson.

The last rites over the remains of Ralph Waldo Emerson took place at Concord on the 30th of April. A special train from Boston carried a large number of people. Many persons were on the street, attracted by the services, but were unable to gain admission to the church where the public ceremonies were held. Almost every building in town bore over its entrance door a large black and white rosette with other sombre draperies. The public buildings were heavily draped, and even the homes of the very poor bore outward marks of grief at the loss of their friend and fellow-townsman.

The services at the house, which were strictly private, occurred at 2-30, and were conducted by Rev. W. H. Furness, of Philadelphia. They were simple in character, and only Mr. Furness took part. The body lay in the front north-east room, in which were gathered the family and close friends of the deceased. The only flowers were contained in three vases on the mantel, and were lilies of the valley, red and white roses, and arbutus. The adjoining room and hall were filled with friends and neighbours.

The poet's wife and daughter Ellen sat near the coffin. Dr. Furness occupied a position in the passage-way, and made a brief and touching address, saying that the peaceful face lying before them only indicated a like quiet of soul within, and reflected its peace and purity while it yet tenanted the body. He then recited Tennyson's "Deserted Home," and repeated from Longfellow words read at that poet's own funeral, a few weeks ago. Appropriate quotations from Scripture followed.

The procession was then formed for the public services at the Unitarian Church, which is but a short distance from the house. The Concord Social Circle led the way, then followed the hearse and pall-bearers:—Charles Emerson and Haven Emerson, nephews of the deceased; Wm. H. Forbes, Emerson's son-in-law; J. Elliott Cabot, Emerson's biographer; Prof. James B. Thayer, of Harvard Law School; Dr. Edward Emerson, Mr. Ralph Forbes, and Mr. W. Thayer, all relatives of the deceased, and following them were a few carriages with the family and intimate friends, among whom were Oliver Wendell Holmes, G. W. Curtis, President Eliot, of Harvard College; Professors Norton, Pierce, Horsford, and Hills, of Cambridge; Mrs. J. T. Fields, representatives of the Boston publishing houses, and many others.

At the church many hundreds of persons were awaiting the arrival of the procession, and all the space, except the reserved pews, were packed. In front of the pulpit were simple decorations, boughs of pine covered the desk, and in their centre was a harp of yellow jonquils, the gift of Miss Louisa M. Alcott. Other floral tributes were an open volume, upon one page on white ground the word "Finis" in blue flowers. This was from the teachers and scholars in the Emerson School. By the sides of the pulpit were white and scarlet geraniums and pine boughs, and high upon the wall a laurel wreath.

Before 3-30 the pall-bearers brought in the plain black walnut coffin, which was placed before the pulpit. The lid was turned back and upon it was put a cluster of richly coloured pansies and a small bouquet of roses. While the coffin was being carried in "Pleyel's Hymn" was rendered on the organ by request of the family of the deceased. Dr. James Freeman Clarke then entered the pulpit. Judge E. Rockwood Hoar remained by the coffin below, and when the congregation became quiet made a brief and pathetic address, his voice many times trembling with emotion.

Mr. Hoar began his tribute with the words: "The beauty of Israel is fallen in its high place." He then spoke of the world-wide sorrow felt at the poet's death and of the special veneration and grief of the townspeople, who considered him their own. "There is nothing to mourn for. That brave and manly life was rounded out to the full length of days; that dying pillow was softened by the sweetest domestic affection, and as he lay down to the sleep which the Lord giveth His beloved, his face was as the face of a child and seemed to give a glimpse of the opening heavens. Wherever the English language is spoken throughout the world his fame is established and secured; from beyond the sea and throughout this great land will come innumerable voices of sorrow for this great public loss. But we, his neighbours and townsmen, feel that he was ours; he was descended from the founders of the town; he chose our village for the place in which his life-long work was to be done; it was to our fields and orchards that his presence gave such value; it was in our streets that children looked up to him with love, and the elders with reverence; he was our ornament and pride. The lofty brow, the home of all wise thoughts and aspirations; those lips of eloquent music; that great soul, which, trusting in God, never lost its hope of immortality; that great heart, to which everything was welcome that belonged to man; that impressible nature, loving and tender and generous, having no repulsion or scorn for anything but meanness and baseness; our friend, brother, father, lover, teacher, inspirer, guide, is gone. There is no more that we can do now than to give this our hail and farewell!"

Judge Hoar's remarks were followed by the congregation singing the hymns "Thy will be done," "I will not fear the fate provided by Thy love." The Rev. Mr. Furness then read selections from the Scriptures.

The Rev. James Freeman Clarke delivered a long and very interesting address upon the life and works of the deceased, after which a feeling prayer was offered by Rev. Howard M. Brown, of Brookline, and the benediction closed the exercises in the church. Immediately before the benediction, Mr. Alcott recited a sonnet he had written for the occasion.

Over an hour was occupied by the passing files of neighbours, friends, and visitors looking for the last time upon the face of the dead poet. The body was robed completely in white, and the face bore a natural and peaceful expression. From the church the procession took its way to the cemetery. The grave was made beneath a tall pine tree upon the hill top to the east of Sleepy Hollow, the upturned sod being concealed by strewings of pine boughs. A border of hemlock spray surrounded the grave and completely lined its sides. The services here were very brief and the casket was soon lowered to its final resting place.

The Rev. Dr. Haskins, a cousin of the family, an Episcopal clergyman, read the Episcopal burial service, and closed with the Lord's Prayer, ending at the words "and deliver us from evil." In this all the people joined. Dr. Haskins then pronounced the benediction. After it was over the grandchildren passed by the open grave and threw flowers into it.

RECOLLECTIONS,

LETTERS,

AND

MISCELLANIES

RELATING TO

EMERSON.

RECOLLECTIONS.

MR. EMERSON'S VISITS TO ENGLAND IN 1833, 1847-8, AND 1872-3.

It was in the month of August, 1833—nearly fifty years ago—that I had the singular good fortune to make the acquaintance of Mr. Emerson, and to enjoy the privilege of several days' intercourse with him. I was then residing in Edinburgh, my native city, and he was on his way home, after his first visit to Europe. He had with him a letter of introduction to a friend of mine, who, luckily for me, was then so much engaged in professional duties, that he was unable to spare even a few hours to do the honours of the old Scottish metropolis; so the young American traveller was handed over to me, and I thus became "an entertainer of angels unawares." In those early days Mr. Emerson was about thirty years of age, and his name was then utterly unknown in the world of letters; for the period to which I refer was anterior, by several years, to his delivery of those remarkable addresses which took by surprise the most thoughtful of his countrymen, as well as of cultivated English readers. Neither had he published any of those essays which afterwards stamped him as the most original thinker America had produced. At that time he was still connected with the Unitarian body in New England, although not in full agreement with it on certain matters of doctrine. On Sunday, the 18th of August, 1833, I heard him deliver a discourse in the Unitarian Chapel, Young Street, Edinburgh, and I remember distinctly the effect which he produced on his hearers. It is almost needless to say that nothing like it had ever been heard by them before, and many of them did not know what to make of it. The originality of his thoughts, and the consummate beauty of the language in which they were clothed, the calm dignity of his bearing, the absence of all oratorical effort, the singular directness and simplicity of his manner, free from the least shadow of dogmatic assumption, made a deep impression on me. Not long before this I had listened to a wonderful sermon by Dr. Chalmers, whose force, and energy, and vehement, but rather turgid eloquence carried, for the moment, all before them—his audience becoming like clay in the hands of the potter. But I must confess that the pregnant thoughts and serene self-possession of the young Boston minister had a greater charm for me than all the rhetorical splendours of Chalmers. His voice was the sweetest, the most winning and penetrating of any I ever heard; nothing like it have I listened to since.

> That music in our hearts we bore,
> Long after it was heard no more.

We visited together the courts of law and other places of interest to a stranger, and ascended Blackford Hill, which commands a fine view of the city from the south. There were thus good opportunities for conversation. He spoke on many subjects connected with life, society, and literature, and with an affluence of thought and fulness of knowledge which surprised and delighted me. I had never before met with any one of so fine and varied culture and with such frank sincerity of speech. There was a graciousness and kind encouragement, too, in his manner, inexpressibly winning to one so much younger than himself; and it was with a feeling almost akin to reverence that I listened to and drank in his high thoughts and ripe wisdom. A refined and delicate courtesy, a kind of spiritual hospitality, so to speak,—the like of which, or anything approaching to which, I have never encountered,—seemed to be a part of his very nature, and inseparable from his "daily walk and conversation." It was not therefore extraordinary,—rather quite a natural result,—that the impression produced on me was intense and powerful.

It is with a feeling of something like pride that I find recorded, in a journal kept at the time, some memoranda of that brief intercourse, written in a strain of youthful, enthusiastic admiration, and of perfectly confident expectancy as to his future—a strain which might at that time have sounded very inflated, but which his subsequent career may be said to have rendered almost tame and inadequate. He spoke much about Coleridge, whom he had just visited at Highgate. I happened then to be reading the prose works of that writer, and these formed a fruitful topic of conversation. He spoke of his "Friend" and "Biographia Literaria" as containing many admirable passages for young thinkers, many valuable advices regarding the pursuit of truth and the right methods to be adopted in its investigation, and the importance of having precise and correct notions on moral and intellectual subjects. He considered that there were single sentences in these two works, which embodied clearer ideas of some of the most subtle of human speculations than are to be met with in the pages of any other thinker. "Let no one, however, expect in these books of Coleridge's anything strictly symmetrical. The works themselves are disjointed, inconsecutive, and totally destitute of all regularity and plan. As Hazlitt, with his usual acuteness, truly said of them—'They are vast prefaces and projects preliminary to immense productions which he was always contemplating, but could never bring himself to execute.'" He spoke of Dr. Channing, Sir James Mackintosh, Goethe's "Wilhelm Meister," and Charles Cotton's translation of Montaigne's "Essays," which he regarded as matchless among translations. "After reading Cotton's racy English,' he said, "Montaigne seems to lose, if you look into him in the original old French."

I find that in an essay on "Books," published in 1860, he says that he prefers reading the ancients in translation. It was a tenet of Goethe's that whatever is really valuable in any work is translateable. "I should as soon think," says he, "of swimming across Charles River when I want to go to Boston, as of reading all my books in originals, when I have them rendered for me in my mother tongue." After Bohn's volumes of translations of the Classics made their appearance, he held that they had done for literature what railroads have done for international intercourse.

Some of Walter Savage Landor's "Imaginary Conversations" he greatly admired—particularly those between Bacon and Richard Hooker, Sir Isaac Newton and Isaac Barrow, and Diogenes and Plato. Although not an admirer of the Utilitarian philosophy, he had some of Jeremy Bentham's hair and a scrap of his handwriting. He asked me if I was in the habit of writing down my thoughts. I said I was not; that reading was my greatest pleasure and solace—*laborum dulce lenimen*. "I advise you," said he, "and other young men, to write down your ideas. I have found my benefit in it. It fixes more firmly in your mind what you know, and what you have acquired, and reveals to you unerringly which of your ideas are vague, and which solid." Of De Quincey, Wordsworth, and Carlyle he spoke many times—especially Carlyle, of whom he expressed the warmest admiration. Some of his articles in the "Edinburgh Review" and "Foreign Quarterly Review" had much struck him—one particularly, entitled "Characteristics"—and the concluding passages of another on German Literature, regarding which he was desirous of speaking to the author. He wished much to meet both Carlyle and Wordsworth: "Am I, who have hung over their works in my chamber at home, not to see these men in the flesh, and thank them, and interchange some thoughts with them, when I am passing their very doors?" He spoke of their "rich thoughts, and rare, noble glimpses of great truths, their struggles to reveal their deepest inspirations, and glorious hopes of the future of humanity—not all at once very apparent, but to be digged out, as it were, reverently and patiently from their works."

There was great and, I remember, almost insuperable difficulty in ascertaining where Mr. Carlyle then lived, and I well remember the pains Mr. Emerson took to get the information; at last, it was obtained from the secretary to the University. "I will be sure to send you, before sailing, an account of my visit to Carlyle and Wordsworth, if I should be fortunate enough to see them." Accordingly, in faithful fulfilment of his promise, he wrote me a letter on the 30th of August, 1833, from Liverpool, giving an account of the interviews he had with both of them. These interviews he has described in his "English Traits," published twenty-three years afterwards, and must be well known to the readers of that best of all books on England. He found that Carlyle had heard of his purpose to visit him from a friend, and, on his arrival, he insisted on dismissing the gig which had been hired to carry him from Dumfries to Craigenputtock—a distance of sixteen or seventeen miles. It was therefore sent back, to return the next day, in time for him to secure his seat in the evening coach for the south. So he spent nearly twenty-four hours with Carlyle and his accomplished wife, who were living in perfect solitude among some desolate hills in the parish of Dunscore—not a person to speak to within seven miles. "I found him one of the most simple and frank of men, and became acquainted with him at once. We walked over several miles of hills, and talked upon all the great questions that interest us most. The comfort of meeting a man of genius is that he speaks sincerely; that he feels himself to be so rich, that he is above the meanness of pretending to knowledge which he has not, and Carlyle does not pretend to have solved the great problems, but rather to be an observer of their solution as it goes forward in the world. I asked him at what religious development the concluding passage in his piece in the 'Edinburgh Review' upon German literature (say five years ago), and some passages in the piece called 'Characteristics,' pointed? He replied that he was not competent to state it even to himself—he waited rather to see. My own feeling was that I had met with men of far less power who had got greater insight into religious truth. He is, as you might guess from his papers, the most catholic of philosophers; he forgives and loves everybody, and wishes each to struggle on in his own place and arrive at his own ends. But his respect for eminent men, or rather his scale of eminence, is about the reverse of the popular scale. Scott, Mackintosh, Jeffrey, Gibbon—even Bacon—are no heroes of his; stranger yet, he hardly admires Socrates, the glory of the Greek world—but Burns, and Samuel Johnson, and Mirabeau, he said interested him, and I suppose whoever else has given himself with all his heart to a leading instinct, and has not *calculated* too much. But I cannot think of sketching even his opinions, or repeating his conversations here. I will cheerfully do it when you visit me in America. He talks finely, seems to love the broad Scotch, and I loved him very much at once. I am afraid he finds his entire solitude tedious, but I could not help congratulating him upon his treasure in his wife, and I hope he will not leave the moors; 'tis so much better for a man of letters to nurse himself in seclusion than to be filed down to the common level by the compliances and imitations of city society. And you have found out the virtues of solitude, I remember, with much pleasure."

The third day afterwards, Mr. Emerson called on Wordsworth at Rydal Mount, and was cordially received, the poet remembering up all his American acquaintance. Here is his description of the interview:—"He had very much to say about the evils of superficial education, both in this country and in mine. He thinks that the intellectual tuition of society is going on, out of all proportion, faster than its moral training, which last is essential to all *education*. He does not wish to hear of schools of tuition; it is the education of circumstances which he values, and much more to this point. He says that he is not in haste to publish more poetry, for many reasons, but that what he has written will be at some time given to the world. He led me out into a walk in his grounds, where he said many thousands of his lines were composed, and repeated to me three beautiful sonnets, which he had just finished, upon the occasion of his recent visit to Fingal's Cave, at Staffa. I hope he will print them speedily. The third is a gem. He was so benevolently anxious to impress upon me my social duties as an American citizen, that he accompanied me near a mile from his house, talking vehemently, and ever and anon stopping short to imprint his words. I noted down some of these when I got to my inn, and you may see them in Boston, Massachusetts, when you will. I enjoyed both my visits highly, and shall always esteem your Britain very highly in love for its wise and good men's sake. I remember with much pleasure my visit to Edinburgh, and my short acquaintance with yourself and your good parents. It will give me very great pleasure to hear from you, to know your thoughts. Every man that ever was born has some that are peculiar. Present my respects to your father and family.—Your friend and servant, R. WALDO EMERSON."

So much with regard to Mr. Emerson's first visit to England. As every one knows, his name, in a very few years, became celebrated in his own country, exercising a remarkable influence in all thoughtful circles.

Mr. Carlyle edited Emerson's first series of Essays published in this country in 1841. In his preface to them he wrote:—" The name of Ralph Emerson is not entirely new in England; distinguished travellers bring us tidings of such a man; fractions of his writings have found their way into the hands of the curious here; fitful hints that there is, in New England, some spiritual notability called Emerson, glide through reviews and magazines. Whether these hints were true or not true, readers are now to judge for themselves a little better. . . . Emerson's writings and speakings amount to something; and yet, hitherto, as seems to me, this Emerson is perhaps far less notable for what he has spoken or done, than for the many things he has not spoken and has forborne to do. With uncommon interest I have learned that this, and in such a never-resting, locomotive country, too, is one of these rare men who have withal the invaluable talent of sitting still! That an educated man, of good gifts and opportunities, after looking at the public arena, and even trying, not with ill success, what its tasks and its prizes might amount to, should retire for long years into rustic obscurity; and amid the all-pervading jingle of dollars and loud chaffering of ambitions and promotions, should quietly, with cheerful deliberateness, sit down to spend *his* life, not in Mammon worship, or the hunt for reputation, influence, place, or any outward advantage whatsoever: this, when we get a notice of it, is a thing worth noting."

The publication, in England, of this and the second series of essays, which took place a year or two later, made his name widely known throughout Great Britain, and thinking persons recognised in him an intellectual leader. Many of his friends were desirous that he should come to England, and deliver courses of lectures similar to those he had given with such signal success in various cities of the United States. In this desire I warmly shared. In the autumn of 1846, a very favourable opportunity presented itself of sending a message to him by a common friend—Mr. Lloyd Garrison—who was then sailing from Liverpool to Boston, and who promised to deliver it himself. I gladly availed myself of the occasion, and on the spur of the moment, just before the ship steamed out of the Mersey, I wrote him a hasty note in pencil, urging him to entertain the project of a lengthened visit to England, and which should embrace the delivery of lectures in some of the chief towns. Before long I received a reply, which was more favourable than I expected. It was full of kind words and reminiscences. " Your suggestion is new and unlooked for, yet opens to me at once so many flattering possibilities, that I shall cheerfully entertain it, and perhaps we may both see it ripen, one day to a fact. Certainly it would be much more practicable and pleasing to me to answer an invitation than to come into your cities and challenge an audience." Some months later (28th February, 1847) he wrote :—" I owe you new thanks for your friendly and earnest attention to the affair of Lectures which you have put me on, but I had not anticipated so prompt an execution of the project as you suggest. Certainly I cannot think of it for April (1847). For September I will think of it, but cannot at present fix anything. I really have not the means of forming an opinion of the expediency of such an attempt. I feel no call to make a visit of literary propagandism in England. All my impulses to work of that kind would rather employ me at home. It would be still more unpleasing to me to put upon a few friends the office of collecting an audience for me, by much advertisement and coaxing. At the same time it would be very agreeable to me to accept any good invitation to read lectures from institutions, or from a number of friendly individuals who sympathised with my studies. But though I possess a good many decisive tokens of interest in my pursuits and way of thinking from sundry British men and women, they are widely sundered persons, and my belief is that in no one city, except perhaps in London, could I find any numerous company to whom my name was favourably known. If I were younger, it would give me great pleasure to come to England and collect my own audience, as I have done at home here ; and I have that confidence in my favourite topics and in my own habits, that I should undertake the affair without the least distrust. But perhaps my ambition does not give to a success of this kind that importance it has had for me. At all events, in England I incline rather to take than to give the challenge. So that you see my project requires great frankness on your part. You must not suffer your own friendly feelings to give the smallest encouragement to the design. . . . You inquire what are the rates of remuneration of lecturers here. . . . I am glad to hear what you tell me of your employments and position. I doubt not life has taught and is teaching us both one lesson. It would be strange, but most agreeable to me, to renew again our brief yet never-forgotten acquaintance of thirteen or fourteen years ago in Edinburgh.— With ever kindest regards."

It was quite characteristic of Mr. Emerson to under-estimate the extent to which his name was known and his writings appreciated in England. No sooner was it announced that he had decided to revisit this country and to read lectures, than (as has been stated in a previous page) applications from every part of the kingdom began to flow in, and in many cases it was found impossible to comply with the wishes of the requisitionists, from a fear of committing him to engagements which might have become burdensome to him. Speaking of the occasion of his second visit to England in "English Traits," he says:—"I did not go very willingly. I am not a good traveller, nor have I found that long journeys yield a fair share of reasonable hours. But the invitation was repeated and pressed at a moment of more leisure, and when I was a little spent by some unusual studies. I wanted a change and a tonic, and England was proposed to me. Besides, there were, at least, the dread attraction and salutary influences of the sea, so I took my berth in the packet ship, 'Washington Irving,' and sailed from Boston on Tuesday, 5th October, 1847."

His friend Carlyle was greatly delighted with the prospect

of again seeing Mr. Emerson. A letter from the latter, announcing the probable time of his sailing, had, by accidental negligence at a country post-office, failed to reach Carlyle in due course, and only turned up near the time of Mr. Emerson's expected arrival, thus depriving his friend of the opportunity of responding. The only thing left to be done was to get the reply delivered to Mr. Emerson as soon as he should land. Knowing that I was in communication with him, and certain to be cognisant of the time of his arrival, Mr. Carlyle wrote me on the subject, and his letter is so delightfully characteristic of his high regard for Mr. Emerson, and his earnest desire to free himself from even the slightest appearance of a want of hospitality, that I must give an extract from it. It is dated Chelsea, 15th October, 1847, just ten days after Mr. Emerson had sailed :—" By a letter I had very lately from Emerson— which had lain, lost and never missed, for above a month in the treacherous post-office of Buxton, where it was called for and denied—I learn that Emerson intended to sail for this country 'about the 1st of October;' and infer, therefore, that probably even now he is near Liverpool or some other of our ports. Treadmill, or other as emphatic admonition, to that scandalous post-master of Buxton! He has put me in extreme risk of doing one of the most unfriendly and every way unpardonable-looking things a man could do! Not knowing in the least to what port Emerson is tending, when he is expected, or what his first engagements are, I find no way of making my word audible to him in time, except that of entrusting it, with solemn charges, to you, as here. Pray do me the favour to contrive in some sure way that Emerson may get hold of that note the instant he lands in England. I shall be permanently grieved otherwise ; shall have failed in a clear duty (were it nothing more) which will never, probably, in my life offer itself again. Do not neglect, I beg much of you ; and, on the whole, if you can, get Emerson put safe into the express train, and shot up hither, as the first road he goes !

That is the result we aim at. But the note itself, at all events, I pray you get that delivered duly, and so do me a very great favour, for which I depend on you." I need scarcely say that these solemn injunctions, so characteristic of Carlyle, were faithfully carried out to the very letter.

The ship reached Liverpool on the 22nd of October, 1847, and Mr. Emerson at once proceeded to Manchester, where I had the pleasure of receiving him at the Victoria Station. After spending a few hours in friendly talk, he was "shot up," as Carlyle had desired, to Chelsea, and at the end of a week returned to Manchester to commence the first of a series of lecturing engagements which had been arranged for him. In a previous page (Memoir, p. 16) I have endeavoured to give the reader some idea (I feel how inadequate it is) of Emerson's manner of reading in public, and its influence on his hearers.

During his stay in Manchester, and just before going to London to pay a round of visits and to lecture, he invited a number of friends from various parts of the country to dine and spend an evening with him at his lodgings in Lower Broughton. His guests were principally young men—ardent, hopeful, enthusiastic moral and religious reformers and visionaries, gathered together from Birmingham, Sheffield, Nottingham, Liverpool, Huddersfield, Newcastle, and other towns. One of them, a man of erratic genius, and of very straitened means (but nevertheless an inveterate smoker), who not many years ago died in a lunatic asylum in New York, trudged on foot all the way from Huddersfield to be present, and next day performed the same feat homeward. He has left behind him a detailed description of this gathering, written in a rather sarcastic spirit, but curious for its life-like sketches of his fellow-guests. One of the finest spirits assembled on that occasion—Henry Sutton, of Nottingham, whose little volume of Poems, in Emerson's opinion, contained pieces worthy of the genius of George Herbert—and who, happily, is still living in our midst, honoured and beloved by his friends—says that the impression left on his mind was that the affair went off admirably, and that all seemed delighted to have had such an opportunity of coming into closer contact with Emerson—that no one could but feel gratified by his kindliness and gentle dignity, and that his conduct and manner were perfect. "Any criticism to the contrary could only excite pity for the writer, if it did not too strongly call forth disgust." It was a memorable symposium. With his fine graciousness of manner and delicate courtesy, Emerson listened with serene amiability, and an ineffably sweet smile to everything his young guests had to say, and made them feel, as was his wont, that *he* was the favoured one of the party, and that *he* specially was imbibing much wisdom and benefit from their discourse. In the course of the evening, being urgently requested to do so, he read his lecture on Plato, then in MS., but now printed in his "Representative Men."

Among the guests who were present at this motley gathering were two—no longer living—of whom I wish to say a few words. One of them was Dr. W. B. Hodgson, late Professor of Political Economy in the University of Edinburgh, who died unexpectedly in Brussels in 1880, lamented by a very large circle of friends. I had known him intimately almost from his boyhood. At the time of Emerson's visit he was proprietor and conductor of the Chorlton High School, Manchester. He was a man of brilliant gifts, a classical scholar of no common mark, and master of several European languages. His kindly nature, extensive knowledge of literature, and conversational powers can never be forgotten by those who knew him. As an after-dinner talker he had few equals. His marvellous memory (for he never forgot anything he had ever read, or heard, or seen), supplied him with an inexhaustible store of witty and humorous stories and anecdotes, sparkling *bon mots*, and an unfailing affluence of apt quotation. No story, however good, could be told by another person in his presence which he was not able to cap on the instant by a better one. In this social field he was *facile princeps*. During his life he rendered most valuable services to the cause of education by his addresses, lectures, and other publications, and by his *vast* (for no other word can in this case be used) correspondence with Educational Reformers, Political Economists, and heads of Schools and Colleges, in every part of the kingdom. I may safely say that, during forty years, he spent, on an average, two or three hours a day, at least, in correspondence.

The other guest to whom I wish to refer was Joseph Neuberg, whom I knew for more than twenty years, and whose memory I cherish for his many admirable qualities of head and heart. He was a highly-cultivated and thoughtful German, born at Würzburg. Mr. Emerson had made his acquaintance at Nottingham, when lecturing there — was, indeed, his guest. Neuberg was a successful merchant, and had recently sustained a severe domestic affliction in the death of his wife. At the time I speak of, he was living with a sister, as his companion, in a beautiful home, looking down upon the Trent and its green meadows. He had ardent literary tastes, was an enthusiastic admirer of Carlyle's writings, and had long wished to become acquainted with him. The gratification of this desire was brought about by the friendly aid of Emerson, who spoke of him to Carlyle in terms of high commendation. Neuberg afterwards proposed to Carlyle to wind up his business and to reside in London, and live on the modest fortune he had made; devoting himself, heart and soul, to his service. This proposal soon became a reality. He finally left Nottingham, after winding up his affairs, and settled in London. From that period up to the time of his death, about fifteen years ago, he was in almost daily communication with Carlyle. His industry was untiring. He made researches for Carlyle in all quarters—often spending days and weeks in the library of the British Museum, unearthing facts and dates from hundreds of obscure and neglected books, manuscripts, and maps, thus saving his friend an endless amount of distasteful drudgery. He would think nothing of spending a whole day in verifying a single fact or date. During the composition of "The Life of Friedrich," his services were of great value, and were fully appreciated by Carlyle. They proceeded together to Germany, and inspected all the battle-fields and places of historical interest described in the Life. He also translated into German the successive volumes of the work. By this arrangement they appeared simultaneously in London and Berlin. Neuberg did not live to translate the last two volumes, which were done by another hand. Carlyle was much grieved when death deprived him of this faithful friend and assistant. In no account of his friend which has yet appeared, has any notice been taken of Neuberg, nor any tribute paid to his memory. In the "Reminiscences" his name once occurs in a parenthesis, but there is no note appended to tell the reader who he was—*Stat nominis umbra*. In "Shooting Niagara; and after?" Carlyle quotes a piece of information furnished to him by Neuberg. Without naming him, he speaks of his informant as "one of the wisest and faithfullest German friends I ever had, a correct observer, and much a lover both of his own country and of mine." In a letter from Carlyle to Mr. Neuberg's sister, written in April, 1867, he says:—"If the bust give you any satisfaction, surely I shall think it, all my days, to have been well worth while! No kinder friend had I in this world; no man of my day, I believe, had so faithful, loyal, and willing a helper as he generously was to me for the last twenty or more years. To look for his like again would be very vain indeed, were I even at the beginning of my course, instead of at the end! A man of fine faculty, too;—decidedly the most intelligent, swift, and skilful, at that kind of work, whom I have ever seen and known of. The memory of him will remain dear and noble to me;—the sudden stroke that has cut away such a friend, in these my otherwise desolate days, may well be sad and heavy to me. But if so to me, what then is it to you and your dear little ones? Alas on this head I must *say* nothing. I will bid you be of courage, pious *courage*, and in all things try to do as you think he would have ordered and wished; which I believe will daily be your best consolation in this sore trial."

During the fortnight in which Mr. Emerson delivered his course of lectures in London, at the Portman Square Literary and Scientific Institution, in the summer of 1848 (referred to at page 15 of the Memoir), I had the honour of being his guest. He had lodgings in the house of Mr. John Chapman, in the Strand—a well-known publisher of those days. As he had been already many weeks in London, he had met a large number of literary and social celebrities, including Rogers, Hallam, Milman, Barry Cornwall, Helps, Clough, Matthew Arnold, Faraday, Owen, Lyell, Carpenter, Mrs. Jameson, Henry Crabb Robinson, Mrs. Somerville, Dickens, Thackeray, Tennyson, and, I believe, Macaulay. He also received invitations from and visited several members of the aristocracy, including the Duchess of Sutherland. Notwithstanding his numerous social engagements, he generally devoted many hours a day to study, retiring to his room immediately after breakfast, and extending the forenoon to three o'clock. The lectures to which I have referred were prepared with much care, as will be seen by his correspondence with myself, prior to my joining him in London. During this visit we went to some of the theatres together—on one evening hearing Jenny Lind, who was then achieving her first triumphs in London. He was very desirous of calling upon Leigh Hunt, and as I had known the latter for many years, and was in the habit of spending an evening with him when business carried me to London, it was proposed that I should take him to Hunt's house. The interview lasted, I think, a couple of hours, and evidently gave great pleasure to both. I have already mentioned that he thought the two finest-mannered literary men he had met

in England were Leigh Hunt and De Quincey. Hunt charmed him by his sprightly, sparkling conversation, overflowing with anecdote and quotation. His courteous and winning manner was on this occasion tempered by a certain delicate reverence, indicating how deeply he felt the honour of being thus sought out by his distinguished visitor. It is singular that Hunt produced a similar impression upon Hawthorne. I venture to give a portion of his description of him—one of the most touching sketches that Hawthorne has written:—
"He was a beautiful old man. In truth, I never saw a finer countenance, either as to the mould of features or the expression, nor any that showed the play of feeling so perfectly. It was like a child's face in this respect. At my first glimpse of him, I discerned that he was old, his long hair being white, and his wrinkles many. It was an aged visage, in short such as I had not at all expected to see, in spite of dates, because his books talk to the reader with the tender vivacity of youth. But when he began to speak, and as he grew more earnest in conversation, I ceased to be sensible of his age; sometimes, indeed, its dusky shadow darkened through the gleam which his sprightly thoughts diffused about his face, but then another flash of youth came out of his eyes, and made an illumination again. I never witnessed such a wonderfully illusive transformation, before or since; and, to this day, trusting only to my recollection, I should find it difficult to decide which was his genuine and stable predicament—youth or age. I have met no Englishman whose manners seemed to me so agreeable— soft, rather than polished, wholly unconventional, the natural growth of a kindly and sensitive disposition, without any reference to rule, or else obedient to some rule so subtle that the nicest observer could not detect the application of it. I felt that no effect upon my mind of what he uttered, no emotion, however transitory, in myself, escaped his notice,—his faculty of observation was so penetrative and delicate. On matters of feeling, and within a certain

depth, you might spare yourself the trouble of utterance, because he already knew what you wanted to say, and perhaps a little more than you would have spoken. There were abundant proofs throughout our interview of an unrepining spirit, resignation, quiet relinquishment of the worldly benefits that were denied him, thankful enjoyment of whatever he had to enjoy, and piety, and hope shining onward into the dark,—all of which gave a reverential cast to the feeling with which we parted from him. I wish that he could have had one full draught of prosperity before he died. At our leave-taking he grasped me warmly by both hands, and seemed as much interested in our whole party as if he had known us for years. All this was genuine feeling, a quick, luxuriant growth out of his heart, which was a soil for flower-seeds of rich and rare varieties, not acorns, but a true heart, nevertheless." The effect produced upon Emerson by his visit to Leigh Hunt was in most respects the same as in the case of Hawthorne, and could not be expressed in more true and touching words than those I have just quoted. He often recurred to the interview, and spoke of it as one of the most delightful he had ever had with a man of letters.

Many interesting places and persons we saw together in London. An evening spent at the house of John Minter Morgan, a wealthy social reformer and associationist, deserves special mention. This gentleman was an amiable, gentle, and sweet-mannered enthusiast, and had written several works well-known in his peculiar field of literature: "Hampden in the Nineteenth Century," "Colloquies on Religion," "The Christian Commonwealth," "Extinction of Pauperism," "The Revolt of the Bees," "The Phœnix Library," a series of works, original and reprinted, on the Renovation and Progress of Society, in Religion, Morality, and Science. It is only necessary to read the titles of these works in order to know the views and opinions of this worthy moral reformer. He had met Emerson somewhere in London, and obtained the promise of an evening. Thereupon was gathered in his large drawing-room an extraordinary assembly, consisting of many of the leading socialists in London. The first part of the evening was spent in the contemplation of a huge coloured revolving view of a series of associated villages and homes, with the most enchanting representations of churches for the cultivation of universal religion, elegant lecture and concert rooms, and theatres,—of ladies and gentlemen walking about in the healthy costumes of the future, their children playing about them, and over all, a sky of unclouded blue. Mr. Morgan, with a long rod, explained to his audience the meaning and significance of all these beautiful objects, and answered many questions put to him by timid believers and admirers, chiefly ladies. After this entertainment the company adjourned to tea and coffee, and after a couple of hours spent in introductions and the conversations naturally flowing therefrom, the party broke up at eleven o'clock. Emerson confessed that he had never before met such a gathering of singular people, and often humorously alluded to it afterwards.

On the day which Mr. Emerson spent in Edinburgh, on his last visit to Europe (May 8th, 1873), he dined at the house of a friend, Dr. William Smith, the translator of many of Fichte's works, and President of the Edinburgh Philosophical Association, who heard him preach in Edinburgh in 1833, and who had listened to his lectures in 1848. At the dinner party he met Lord Neaves,* Dr. W. B.

---

* Lord Neaves was a distinguished member of the Scottish bench, and a man of fine culture, a recognised wit and humourist, and of the most genial disposition; he was a general favourite in Edinburgh social circles. He was the author of many songs and verses, social and scientific, contributed to "Blackwood's Magazine." These have been collected, and have gone through several editions. Some of these verses had quite a renown at the time of their publication. Among them may be named "The Origin of Species," "The Permissive Bill," "I'm very fond of Water," "Hilli-onnee," "Stuart Mill on Mind and Matter," "Let us all be unhappy on Sunday," and others.

Hodgson,[*] and the widow of Dr. Samuel Brown, who had been his host in 1847-8, and a few other friends. He was greatly delighted with the brilliant fire of repartee and wit which was kept up between Lord Neaves and Dr. Hodgson, as well as of the songs of the former, who sang not a few; and he frequently referred to this "wit combat" on his visit to me a few days later. In a scrapbook of the son of his Edinburgh host he inscribed this memorial of his visit. "After a happy evening with excellent company."—R. WALDO EMERSON. 8th May, 1873. On the evening of his arrival (7th May) he met a large party of notabilities in the house of Professor Fraser. A characteristic incident relating to this visit is worth recording. His host, Dr. Smith, thus relates it: "On the 8th I drove him for some time about the city; Miss Emerson, being rather indisposed, remained at the hotel. In the course of our drive we stopped at the shop of a worthy tradesman in Nicholson-street, who is an enthusiastic admirer of E. I had been informed that he had been making anxious inquiries about E.'s place of abode and the probable time of his departure, so that he might have a chance of getting a glimpse of his hero. I alighted, and entering the shop said, ' Mr. ——, Mr. Emerson is at the door, and will be glad to see you for a few minutes.' You may imagine his delight at this unexpected fulfilment of his wishes. The five minutes were well spent, and I have no doubt are a cherished memory."

He spent the last two days of this his final visit to England, under my roof, along with his devoted daughter, Ellen. This afforded an opportunity of bringing together many of his old friends and hearers of 1847-8, whom he was well pleased to meet. To every one he gave a few minutes, and the stream of conversation flowed on for several hours. After all the guests had departed, he indulged in a cigar, and expressed

[*] Late Professor of Political Economy in the University of Edinburgh, already referred to.

his gratification at having met so many "good people," as he called them. "Would that I could have held converse with each for half-an-hour!" A capital *bon mot*, related by him on this occasion, must here be recorded. It would have rejoiced the heart of dear Charles Lamb. Speaking of a convivial club, of which he was a member, having ceased and dispersed for many years, it was thought desirable that the survivors should once more assemble, and revive their old recollections. An interval of ten years had meanwhile elapsed. While the wine was circulating, someone proposed that the society should have a gathering every ten years. Mr. Appleton, one of the company, instantly said, "Then it should have the title of a Dutch picture, ' Boors Drinking' after Teniers " (ten years). His last hours in Liverpool, before sailing, were spent with Mr. R. C. Hall, an old friend and admirer.

It has often struck me that the "marble self-possession" of Emerson, his perfect reliance upon his own genius and intuitions, his grand self-dependence, which no passing excitement could disturb or shake for a moment; and his steadfast belief in the ultimate sovereignty of righteousness and truth, are well indicated in the following remarkable lines, written by an old English poet early in the seventeenth century— Samuel Daniel :—

> One who of such a height hath built his mind,
> And reared the dwelling of his thoughts so strong,
> As neither fear nor hope can shake the frame
> Of his resolvéd powers,   .   .   .
> .   .   .   .   nor pierce to wrong
> His settled peace, nor to disturb the same.
> .   .   .   .
> And with how free an eye doth he look down
> Upon these lower regions of turmoil,
> Where all these storms of passion vainly beat
> On flesh and blood ; where honour, power, renown,
> Are only gay afflictions, golden toil ;
> Where greatness stands upon as feeble feet
> As frailty doth, and only great doth seem
> To little minds, who do it so esteem.

.   .   .   .   who hath prepared
A rest for his desires ; and sees all things
Beneath him ; and hath learned this book of man,
Full of the notes of frailty ; and compared
The best of glory with her sufferings :
.   .   .   inured to any hue
The world can cast ; that cannot cast that mind
Out of its form of goodness ; that doth see
Both what the best and worst of earth can be ;

.   .   .   .

Which makes, that whatsoever here befals,
He in the region of himself remains."

CORRESPONDENCE.

Emerson to Carlyle on "The Life of Friedrich" and the American Civil War.

"*Concord, 1st May, 1859.*

"The book [the first volume of 'The Life of Friedrich'] came, with its irresistible inscription, so that I am all tenderness and all but tears. The book, too, is sovereignly written. I think you the true inventor of the stereoscope, as having exhibited that art in style long before we had yet heard of it in drawing. The letter came also. Every child of mine knows from far that handwriting, and brings it home with speed. . . . You hug yourself on missing the illusion of children, and must be pitied as having one glittering toy the less. I am a victim all my days to certain graces of form and behaviour, and can never come into equilibrium. Now I am fooled by my own young people, and grow old contented. The heedless children suddenly take the keenest hold on life, and foolish papas cling to the world on their account, as never on their own. Out of sympathy, we *make believe* to value the prizes of their ambition and hope. My two girls, pupils once or now of Agassiz, are good, healthy, apprehensive, decided young people, who love life. My boy divides his time between Cicero and cricket,—knows his boat, the birds, and Walter Scott, verse and prose, through and through,—and will go to college next year. Sam Ward and I tickled each other the other day, in looking over a very good company of young people, by finding in the new comers a marked improvement on their parents. There, I flatter myself, I see some emerging of our people from the prison of their politics. . . . I am so glad to find myself speaking once more to you, that I mean to persist in the practice. Be as glad as you have been. You and I shall not know each other, on this platform, as long as we have known. A correspondent even of twenty-five years should not be disused unless through some fatal event. Life is too short, and with all our poetry and morals too indigent, to allow such sacrifices. Eyes so old and weary, and which have learned to look on so much, are gathering an hourly harvest; and I cannot spare what on noble terms is offered me. . . ."

"Concord, 1861.

" Here has come into the country, three or four months ago, another volume of your 'History of Friedrich,' infinitely the wittiest book that ever was written ;—a book that one would think the English people would rise up in mass and thank the author for by cordial acclamation, and signify, by crowning him with oak leaves, their joy that such a head existed among them, and sympathising and much-reading America would make a new treaty, or send a Minister Extraordinary to offer congratulation of honouring delight to England in acknowledgment of this donation ;—a book holding so many memorable and heroic facts, working directly on practice, with new heroes, things unnoticed before—the German Plutarch (now that we have exhausted the Greek and Roman and the British Plutarchs),—with a range, too, of thought and wisdom, so large and so elastic, not so much applying as inculcating to every need and sensibility of man,—that we do not read a stereotype page,—rather we see the eyes of the writer looking into ours ; mark his behaviour, humming, chuckling,—with under tones and trumpet tones, and long commanding glances, stereoscoping every figure that passes, and every hill, river, road, hammock, and pebble in the long perspective—with its wonderful system of mnemonics, whereby great and insignificant men are marked and modelled in memory by what they were, had, and did. . . . And, withal, a book that is a Judgment Day for its moral verdict on the men and nations and manners of modern times. And this book makes no noise. I have hardly seen a notice of it in any newspaper or journal, and you would think there was no such book. I am not aware that Mr. Buchanan has sent a special messenger to Cheyne Row, Chelsea, or that Mr. Dallas had been instructed to assure Mr. Carlyle of his distinguished consideration. But the secret wits and hearts of men take note of it, not the less surely. They have said nothing lately in praise of the air, or of fire, or of the blooming of love ; and yet, I suppose, they are sensible of these, and not less of this book, which is like these."

"*Concord, 8th December, 1862.*

" Long ago, as soon as swift steamers could bring the new book across the sea, I received the third volume of 'Friedrich' with your autograph inscription, and read it with joy. Not a word went to the beloved author, for I do not write or think. I would wait perhaps for happier days, as our President Lincoln will not even emancipate slaves until on the heels of a victory, or the semblance of such. But he waited in vain for his triumph, nor dare I in my heavy months expect bright days.

" The book was heartily grateful, and square to the author's imperial scale. You have lighted the glooms, and engineered away the pits, whereof you poetically pleased yourself with complaining, in your sometime letter to me, clean out of it, and have let sunshine and pure air enfold the scene. First, I read it honestly through for the history ; then I pause and speculate on the muse that inspires, and the friend that reports it. 'Tis sovereignly written, above all literature. . . . I find, as ever in your books, that one man has deserved well of mankind for restoring the scholar's profession to its highest use and dignity. I find also that you are very wilful, and have made a covenant with your eyes that they shall not see anything you do not wish they should. But I was heartily glad to read somewhere that your book was nearly finished in the manuscript, for I would wish you to sit and taste your fame, if that were not contrary to the law of Olympus. My joints ache to think of your rugged labour. Now that you have conquered to yourself such a huge kingdom among men, can you not give yourself breath, and chat a little—an *Emeritus* in the Eternal University—and write a gossiping letter to an old American friend or so? Alas, I own that I have no right to say this last, I who write never. Here we read no books. The war is our sole and doleful instructor. All our bright young men go into it, to be misused and sacrificed by incapable leaders. One lesson they all learn; to hate slavery, *deterrima causa!* But the issue does not yet appear. We must get ourselves morally right. Nobody can help us. 'Tis of no account what England or France may do. Unless backed by our profligate parties, their action would be nugatory, and, if so backed, the worst. But even the war is better than the degrading and descending politics that preceded it for decades of years; and our legislation has made great strides, and if we can stave off that fury of trade which rushes to peace, at the cost of replacing the South in the *status ante bellum*, we can, with something more of courage, leave the problem to another score of years—free labour to fight with the beast, and see if bales, barrels, and baskets cannot find out that thus they pass more commodiously and surely to their ports, through free hands than through barbarians."

"*Concord, 26th Sept., 1864.*

"I had received in July the fourth volume of 'Friedrich,' and it was my best reading in the summer, and for weeks my only reading. One fact was paramount in all the good I drew from it, that whomsoever many years had used and worn, they had not yet broken any fibre of your force;—a pure joy to me who abhor the inroads which time makes on me and my friends. To live too long is the capital misfortune, and I sometimes think if we shall not parry it by better art of living, we shall learn to include in our morals some balder control of the facts. I read once that Jacobi declared that he had some thoughts which,—if he should entertain them,—would put him to death ; and perhaps we have weapons in our intellectual armoury that are to save us from disgrace and impertinent relation to the world we live in. But this book will excuse you from any unseemly haste to make up your accounts, nay, holds you to fulfil your career with all amplitude and calmness. I found joy and pride in it, and discovered a golden chain of continuity not often seen in the works of men, apprising me that one good head and great heart remained in England immovable,—superior to his own eccentricities and perversities,—nay, wearing these, I can well believe, as a jaunty coat or red cockade to defy or mislead idlers, for the better securing his own peace and the very ends which the idlers fancy he resists. England's lease of power is good during his days. I have in these last years lamented that you had not made the visit to America, which in earlier years you projected or favoured. It would have made it impossible that your name should be cited for one moment on the side of the enemies of mankind. Ten days' residence in this country would have made you the organ of the sanity of England and Europe to us and to them, and have shown you the necessities and aspirations which struggle up in our free states, which, as yet, have no organ to others and are ill or unsteadily articulated here. In our to-day's division of Republican and Democrat it is certain that the American nationality lies in the Republican party (mixed and multiform though that party be), and I hold it not less certain that, viewing all the nationalities of the world, the battle of Humanity is at this hour in America. A few days here would show you the disgusting composition of the other party which within the Union resists the national action. Take from it the wild Irish element, imported in the last twenty-five years into this country, and led by Romish priests, who sympathise of course with despotism, and you would bereave it of all its numerical strength. A man intelligent and virtuous is not to be found on that side.

"Ah! how gladly I would enlist you with your thunderbolt on our part! How gladly enlist the wise, thoughtful, efficient pens and voices of England! We want England and Europe to hold our people staunch to their best tendency. Are English of this day incapable of a great sentiment? Can they not leave cavilling at petty failures and bad manners, and at the dunce part (always the largest part in human affairs), and leap to the suggestions and finger-pointing of the gods, which, above the understanding, feed the hopes and guide the wills of men? This war has been conducted over the heads of all the actors in it, and the foolish terrors,—'What shall we do with the negro?' 'the entire black population is coming North to be fed,' &c., have strangely ended in the fact that the black refuses to leave his climate; gets his living and the living of his employer there, as he has always done; is the natural ally and soldier of the Republic in that climate; now takes the place of 200,000 white soldiers; and will be, as the conquest of the country proceeds, its garrison, till Peace without Slavery returns. Slaveholders in London have filled English ears with their wishes and perhaps beliefs; and our people, generals and politicians, have carried the like, at first, to the war, until corrected by irresistible experience. I shall always respect War hereafter. The cost of life, the dreary havoc of comfort and time, are overpaid by the vistas it opens of eternal life, eternal law, reconstructing and uplifting Society,—breaks up the old horizon, and we see through the rifts a wider. The dismal Malthus, the dismal De Bow, have had their night. Our Census of 1860, and the war, are poems which will, in the next age, inspire a genius like your own.

" I hate to write you a newspaper, but, in these times, 'tis wonderful what sublime lessons I have once and again read on the bulletin boards in the streets. Everybody has been wrong in his guess, except good women, who never despair of the ideal right."

LETTERS TO A. IRELAND.

"*Liverpool, 30th August, 1833*" (before sailing for America).— Extracts from this letter, describing his first interviews with Carlyle and Wordsworth, will be found at page 53, "Recollections."

"*Concord, 28th Dec., 1846.*— I was very glad to be reminded by your concise note, written on shipboard and conveyed to me by Mr. Garrison, of our brief intercourse thirteen years ago, and which it seems has not yet quite ended. Your affectionate expressions towards me and my friends are very grateful to me; and, indeed, what better thing do men or angels know of than an enduring kindness? In regard to your inquiry whether I shall visit England now or soon, the suggestion is new and unlooked for, yet opens to me at once so many flattering possibilities that I shall cheerfully entertain it, and, perhaps, we may both see it ripen one day to a fact. Certainly it would be much more practicable and pleasant to me to answer an invitation, than to come into your cities and challenge an audience. You have been slower to visit Mr. Wordsworth than I was, but, according to all testimonies, he retains his vigour and his social accomplishments. He could not now remember me in my short and unconnected visit, or I might easily send him assurances, from me and many others also unknown to him, of a regard that could not fail to gratify him.—With the best wishes of these days, &c."

The next letter from him *(Concord, 28th February, 1847,)* will be found at page 57 in "Recollections."

"*Concord, 1st April, 1847.*—My townsman, E. Rockwood Hoar, Esq., is ordered by his physicians to quit his professional duties for a time, and to travel for his health. Mr. Hoar is an eminent practitioner at the Massachusetts Bar, and was lately a member of our State Senate. As he proposes to visit Manchester in his route, I use the opportunity to beg you to introduce him to the Athenæum, and to give him any local information that you may think may be useful to him.—Yours with great regard."

"*Concord, 31st July, 1847.*—I owe you hearty thanks for your effective attention to my affair, which was attractive enough to me in the first proposition, and certainly assumes in your hands a feasible shape. I have a good deal of domestic immoveableness—being fastened down by wife and children, by books and studies, by pear trees and apple trees—but after much hesitation can find no sufficient resistance to this animating invitation, and I decide to go to England in the autumn. I think to leave home about the 1st October, perhaps in the steamer, but more probably in the sailing packet which leaves Boston for Liverpool on the 5th of each month; and, at any rate, shall expect to be in England before the 1st November. From the 1st November, I will take your advice as to the best order of fulfilling those engagements you offer me at Manchester, Sheffield, and Leeds. In regard to the subjects of my lectures, I hope to send you by the next steamer some programme or sketch of programme that may serve a general purpose. I could more easily furnish myself for so 'numerous' a course as seems to offer itself if there were any means of preventing your newspaper reporters from publishing such ample transcripts as I notice (in the 'Examiner' you were so good as to send me) of Mr. Marston's lectures. But I will see what I have to say. Meantime, I beg you not to give yourself any further pains in this matter, which I fear has already cost you much. It will give me pleasure to speak to bodies of your English people, but I am sure it will give me much more to meet with yourself and other honoured individuals in private'; and I see well that, if there were no lecturing, I should not fail to find a solid benefit in the visit.—With great regard."

"*Concord, 30th Sept., 1847.*—I have decided, after a little hesitation and advising with better sailors than myself, to follow my inclination in taking passage in a ship, and not in the steamer. I have engaged a berth in the 'Washington Irving,' which leaves Boston for Liverpool next Tuesday, 5th October. The owners are confident that, with ordinary fortune, we shall arrive in Liverpool in twenty days. But I shall not complain if the voyage should be a little longer. . . . I shall probably think it best to go directly to Manchester to meet yourself, and to settle with you the plan of my little campaign. I suppose that I shall be ready to read lectures at once as soon as the proper notices can be given; or, if more time is required by the institutes, I can go to London, and make a short visit before I begin. I know that I ought to have sent you some synopsis long ago, but it has never been quite certain to me what I could promise, as I have been endeavouring to complete some lectures not even yet quite finished. I think I will now reserve my table of contents until I see you.—Yours, with great regard."

"*Edinburgh, 17th February, 1848.*—Some friends here with me to read my lecture on Plato to the Phil. Society, on Saturday night, at half-past eight o'clock. It lies in one of my bureau drawers at Mrs. Massey's. Now will you proceed with beneficent action at once to Fenny-street, demand a candle, and open the various newspaper envelopes in my drawers until you eliminate and extort 'Plato,' and send it by post immediately to me, care of Dr. Brown, 1, Cuthbert's Glebe

Edinbro'? The good Misses Massey will assist your search, and yourself will reward your pains. I have seen your father and mother, and Mr. Chambers, and others your friends, and all your despatches and benefits have safely arrived.—Ever yours."

"*Ambleside, 29th Feby., 1848.*—Here am I for one day more at Miss Martineau's house. I had fully intended to set out for Manchester this morning; but let myself be over-persuaded by some hospitable friends yesterday, to stay to-day and see the mountains. I had the best visit at Edinburgh, where I parted with your kindest mother last Sunday p.m.; and on Monday, with Dr. Brown and De Quincey, at the station on my way northward. Yesterday I spent a valuable hour, and perhaps a half more, with Mr. Wordsworth, who is in sound health at seventy-seven years, and was full of talk. He would even have walked on my way with me towards Miss Martineau's, but it began to rain, and I would not suffer it.—Ever, with best wishes."

"*London, 142, Strand, 7th March, 1848.*—I am well enough domiciliated here, and am awaiting your visit. . . . I am beginning to see London shows, but, as everywhere, find the morning too precious to go abroad in, and am prone to lengthen the morning till three o'clock. I have seen Carlyle one good day, and, as you ask it, I will send you some good token of him, of this day or a better. But now for another change. . . .—Yours affectionately."

"*142, Strand, London, 9th March, 1848.*—I find him (Carlyle) full of strong discourse. He is in the best humour at the events in France. For the first time in his life he takes in a daily paper—the *Times*—and yet I think he has not much confidence in the ability of the French to carry such great points as they have to carry. He interests himself a good deal in the Chartists, and in politics generally, though with abundant contempt for what is called *political*. He talks away on a variety of matters, on London, on the Universities, on Church and State, on all notable persons, on the delusion that is called Art, on the Sand novels, &c., &c. I think him a most valuable companion, and speaking the best opinions one is likely to hear in this nation. It is by no means easy to talk with him, but there is little need of that, as he enjoys his pictures and his indignations highly. The guiding genius of the man, and what constitutes his superiority over other men of letters, is his commanding sense of justice and incessant demand for sincerity. And I cannot help thinking that he has more books, or at least one more book to write, of more efficiency than any he has written. I expect your promised visit as soon as the hard work is over.—Yours ever."

"*London, 3rd April, 1848.*—I had hoped to have seen you here ere this. My London adventures already make too long a story to write. I spend my time not quite unprofitably, but in a way that must soon have an end, or it would make an end of my comfort. Yet I cannot decline these valued opportunities of seeing men and things which are offered me here. Excepting Tennyson, I believe, I have seen all the literary and many of the political notabilities who interested me. On Thursday last, I went to Oxford, and spent two days and more, very agreeably there, and made the acquaintance of many good men. I have not quite yet decided how long to stay, or whither next to go, but soon must. I carried our good friend Neuberg, the other night, to Carlyle, who was in better mood than usual. I have a good chamber for you here, waiting your advent, and am ever yours. I doubt about Paris a little, being very impatient to be at home and at work."

"*142, Strand, 13th April, 1848.*—Some friends are taking steps here to find me an audience in London, if only

I were ready—and if I do this thing, I must perhaps be too late for you in M. and L. Never ask such a tardy workman as I when his wares will be finished. Meantime I am very industrious, eat a great many dinners, hear a great many lectures, see many persons, many things, go to clubs, theatres, and soirees, receive good letters, through your hands, from home, and get on a line or two in my literary tasks every day. I have never gone to Bristol, Cheltenham, and Exeter, though reminded of my privilege. The London day is not long enough for its manifold deed, and I leave my letters long unanswered. I received with thanks the good 'Examiners.' The last is gone to Boston. I sent you a new 'Mass. Quarterly Review,' but it could not go by post, I found too late, because I had written your name on it.—With kindest remembrances to your friends, I remain, yours faithfully."

"*London, 142, Strand, 3rd May, 1848.*—I have stayed in London a great while, yet have not quite finished my visit. I am going to Paris, I think, on Saturday, and mean to stay there but a short time, as it is decided, almost against me, that I shall read lectures here three weeks hence. Ah, if I knew what to call those lectures! they have grown from day to day and have not yet a name. But the indecision whilst I have been writing here, whether to read or not, and which I had once decided NO, has left me quite unable to send you any word to Manchester. . . . It will also be too late at Manchester for any of those private classes which hovered in your friendly imagination. Besides it is late in the year, and it will be high time for me to set my slow sail for the Capes of Massachusetts. In my short and crowded days here I have given you no account of myself, yet I have found London rich and great, quite equal to its old fame. I have seen a large number of interesting persons, and I suppose the best things—the Parliament, Oxford, the British Museum, Kew

Gardens, the Scientific Societies, the Clubhouses, the Theatres, and so forth. I attend Mr. Owen's lectures at the Royal College of Surgeons; Faraday, at the Royal Institution; Lyell, Sedgwick, Buckland, Forbes, I hear at the Geologic Society; and two nights ago I dined with the Antiquaries, and discussed Shakspeare with Mr. Collier. Dr. Carpenter has shown me his microscopes, Sir Henry Delabeche his geologic museum, and I have really owed many valuable hours to the scientific bodies. Now the Picture Galleries are open, and I have begun to see pictures and artists. It is very easy to see that London would last an inquisitive man a good while, and find him in new studies, but the miscellany is distracting, and quiet countrymen will soon have enough of dining out and of shilling-shows. Yet I value all my new experience, and doubtless shall not wish it less when I am safe in my woods again. In Paris I shall remain three weeks to see the revolution, and to air my nouns and verbs. Mr. Bancroft, who has just returned, takes the most favourable views of their politics, and says the workmen have quite got through all scheme [*sic*] of asking Government to find them labour, repudiate the whole plan, &c. By the last steamer I had no letters from home; if the letters of the due ship come to you, speed them to your ever obliged and grateful."

"*London, Tuesday, 11th July, 1848.*—It now appears certain that I cannot reach Manchester [on his way to Liverpool], do what I can, before 9-4 p.m. on Thursday. So you must give me tea and toast and a bed that night, and despatch me early next morning to Liverpool, where Mrs. Paulet has always been promised the homage of a day. I am very sorry that I am so late and crowded and speedy; 'tis the inevitable fate of my nation. But I could not go without a call at Chatsworth, which I must report to some friends at home, and I stop at Coventry one night first. I have just got home from Stonehenge, whither I went with Carlyle, and Chapman has made out the plan of my new journey to you the best he could.—Yours ever."

"*Concord, 5th July, 1849.*—You will think I died and was buried soon after I left Manchester. No, I escaped the sea and survive until this day, but with no studies or fortunes worth transmitting news of so far; yet not despairing, one of these days, to send you something. But here is my friend, Rev. James Freeman Clarke, an excellent and accomplished man, who can tell you of every good thing in Boston and America, and whom you must furnish with good tidings to me of all your circle.—Yours affectionately."

"*Concord, 12th May, 1850.*—I received many weeks ago a note from you for which I found no answer,—I am sorry for it,—and so sent none. I am so disconnected from all the common systems of lucrative work, that when I hear of an applicant I inquire of other people if there is room. Mr. Greeley (of N.Y.) said, 'None for literary work; we refuse such applications in great numbers.' Rev. Dr. Furness, of Philadelphia, said, 'I always advise the Englishman to come; I know of so many instances of success.' My belief is that there is, for all men of energy, much more room and opportunity here than with you; but almost no more promise here than with you for any infirmity. In the case of your friend, I should think it not wise,—from my impressions of his tendencies and turn of mind,—to make the adventure. I saw him but little, and learned something of him from his friends, the Fishers,—I saw no writing, heard no public speaking, and have no knowledge of what public talent he possesses; but he did not inspire me with any confidence in his good sense, or in his reasonable expectations from society. So I only praise the more your and Mr. Fisher's generous fidelity to him. I was very glad to see your hand

and name, and you must not fail to write me again when you have the like application to make for another person. 'Tis likely I may give you a much better answer. But mainly I look and shall not cease to look for your own arrival, though late, yet sure, it must be, on your tour of observation. Mr. Lawrence, I see, tells you once a month, in London, that 'we are a great nation,' and my dear Carlyle tells you that we are a very dull one; but Nature never disappoints, and our square miles and the amount of human labour here are incontestable, and will interest all your taste, intelligence, and humanity. Forgive me that I never write. My eyes are not good, and I write no letter that is not imperative. I remember you at all times with kindest thankfulness. . . . I heard with joy that E—— was well placed, to command his time and studies. Of Mr. B——, too, his paper brought me good news. And Mr. Kell, of Huddersfield, gave me good tidings of others of your friends.—Yours affectionately."

"*Concord, April 26, 1869.*—Unless I knew your generosity . . . I should hesitate to write a line to you after such unpardonable intervals, lest, if you have not forgotten my handwriting, you should burn it unread. But now I have two commanding motives which break down even my chronic and constitutional reluctance to write a letter. In the first place, a pretty good acquaintance with the brave book you sent me,*—I dare not count how many months ago,—and whose examination even I was long forced to postpone, mainly on account of tasks which have closely succeeded each other ever since October until now, and partly, also, because you had forgotten how much twenty-one or two years have damaged my eyes since I saw you, so that they now refuse to read a type so fine and solid as that of this book, unless in the most favourable circumstances. Polite friends

---

* Mr. Emerson here refers to a volume printed by me in 1868—a labour of love—a " Bibliographical List of the Writings of Charles Lamb, and of the voluminous Works of William Hazlitt and Leigh Hunt."

assure me that it is only because I have darkened my house with a grove of trees, which allow easy reading in my library only in the brightest days. But, at last, I have read much in this pleasant book of justice and love, and can willingly join in the general thanks of scholars to you for this work of loyalty and good taste, so thoroughly and accurately performed, that it will be the *liber veritatis* and *liber studiorum* for all lovers of Lamb and Hazlitt and Hunt, now and hereafter. . . . My second motive for the pen to-day is that my friends, Mr. and Mrs. Fields, who know so many of your English friends, but have never seen yourself, are departing in a couple of days for England and France and Switzerland, and I desire to make it certain that you and they shall meet. You and they have many good qualities in common, and among them the singular eccentricity of an eminent goodwill and helpfulness to me. If it is possible, I hope that Mrs. Ireland and Mrs. Fields may meet, that I may have new information to add to all I drew from the valued photograph you sent me. Miss Mabel Lowell, Mr. J. R. Lowell's only daughter, is of the Fields' party in their tour. I should like well to see you and your Manchester again, you and your household, and to know the history of many of those who surrounded you in 1847-8. Mr. Bright has been at last placed as you anticipated and wished, and the world thinks of Mr. Cobden as you and your friends did. With Mr. W. E. Forster and Mr. Rawlins I have had some communication. . . . All your political friends have been ours, and I wish you will keep them so. But one duty you have left undone, which is to make your own visit to these States, and I shall expect you till you come. Be assured you shall find a hearty welcome in this house.—Yours ever affectionately."

"*Concord, 19th January, 1872.*—I wish that my son-in-law, Col. W. H. Forbes, and my daughter (Edith), his wife, should not fail to see you if they reach Manchester in their passage through England to the continent. They know well your steadfast goodwill and good action at one time, and at all times to me and to my friends, and I have charged them not to fail at seeing you on their way, or else certainly on their return through England. You must show them the specialties of your great city, and you must make them acquainted with Mrs. Ireland, whom I have never seen, though I keep her photograph. Tell them, I pray you, all that I should hear from you, and believe me, ever yours affectionately."

"*Oxford, 1st May, 1872, House of Professor Max Müller.*—It seems that I have been travelling too fast for your letters to catch me. To-day I have received yours of 29th April, and rush to say with thankfulness and regret that my day for reaching Manchester should be the 12th May, and that I will come to you then at Bowdon. Meantime, for Mr. Brown, of Selkirk, I think with gratitude to him that it will be safer for such swift travellers as my daughter and I must be, that it will be best not to trouble him with our swiftness, but to sit down at Kennedy's Hotel, in Edinburgh, and trust to the ordinary resources for our visit to the important points, and I will try to express our thanks to him for his kindest offices. I am sorry to be so tardy with my acknowledgments, and am just now waited for by my hospitable Professor Müller to go to the colleges.—In great haste, but greater love, I remain."

"*Edinburgh, Kennedy's Hotel, 8th May, 1873.*—My best thanks for your affectionate care for me and mine. Ellen tells me that the result of her arithmetic and dates is that we shall arrive at Manchester at 5-20 on Monday from the Lakes, and that I will stay till Wednesday with you, and Ellen will go to Liverpool on Tuesday noon, such are her necessities. Continue, I pray you, your loving-kindness to me and mine. With my greetings to Mrs. Ireland.—Yours ever faithfully."

Mr. Moncure D. Conway.

I consider it due to my friend, Mr. Moncure D. Conway, to give here the letter of introduction which he brought to me from Emerson in 1863. Through the study of his writings he had been led to abandon the creed in which he was reared, and to turn against the institution of slavery prevailing in Virginia. His father was a planter and slave-owner in that State, and the change which came over his son led to their alienation, and to his departure from the paternal home. By Emerson's advice he went to Cambridge University, and entered the Divinity College, connected with Harvard University. His object was to be near his master, and to know more of the man through whom his life had been revolutionised. "Now and then he came at the solicitation of the students to pass an evening in conversation with them or to read an essay. On one occasion, when it was announced that he was to read a lecture at Concord, the Emersonians collected in some force and drove in sleighs by night over the twenty miles to hear him. The lecture had been postponed, but the philosopher took us to his house, and we found in his conversation ample compensation for our disappointment. He treated those present as the guests of his thoughts, with an imperial hospitality, and the questions and answers of the youthful inquirers must have convinced him that if the old circle of Concord had broken up, it was only into divers circles with other centres. Within the next few years his influence in the Divinity College had so increased that he might have been regarded as an ungowned professor; and it will not seem surprising to those who remember those days that he should since have been brought into official relations with the University. A great deal of my time was passed at Concord; Thoreau, Miss Peabody, Ellery Channing, and one or two others of the old fraternity were still there, and the society was very attractive. There were courses of lectures given in the village by eminent gentlemen, and Mr. Emerson's open evenings preserved the literary character of the society. The motley group described by Hawthorne were no longer seen crowding in the streets of Concord, but there were to be frequently met strange faces which, as they passed, the villagers were apt to note with the surmise that they might be famous men from far-off places."

Mr. Conway ultimately settled as a minister in Boston. In 1863 he came to London, and afterwards succeeded to the pastorate of Mr. W. J. Fox's congregation at South Place, Finsbury, a position which he still holds. Mr. Conway has contributed many valuable papers on Emerson and other subjects to "Fraser's Magazine," between 1864 and 1874, and he is a frequent writer in other periodicals. Several books from his pen have made their mark, and are well known and appreciated—" Republican Superstitions;" "The Earthward Pilgrimage;" Sacred Anthology, being Selections from Oriental Scriptures;" an elaborate "History of Demonology," in two vols.; " Legend of the Wandering Jew;" "Thomas Carlyle: Recollections of Seventeen Years' Intercourse;" "Address on John Stuart Mill;" &c., &c. Mr. Conway's abilities and acquirements have gradually secured for him and his admirable wife a very large circle of friends in London, which includes many of the most distinguished men and women of letters, and artists.

Letter Introducing Mr. Conway.

"*Concord, 9th April, 1863.*

"Mr. Moncure D. Conway, a valued neighbour of mine, and a man full of public and private virtues, goes to England just now, having, as I understand, both inward and outward provocation to defend the cause of America there. I can assure you, out of much knowledge, that he is very competent to this duty, if it be one. He is a Virginian by birth and breeding; and now for many years a Northerner in residence and in sentiment. He is a man of excellent ability in speaking and writing, and I grudge to spare his usefulness at home even to a contingency so important as the correcting of opinion in England. In making you acquainted with Mr. Conway, I charge him to remind you that the first moment of American peace will be the best time for you to come over and pay us and me a long promised visit."

MISCELLANEOUS RECORDS.

EMERSON'S BOYHOOD.

Rufus Dawes, who knew Emerson as a boy, gives us in his "Boyhood Memoirs" (1843) a sight of the boy when he was about ten years old :—" It is eight o'clock a.m. ; and the thin gentleman in black, with a small jointed cane under his arm, his eyes deeply sunken in his head, has asked that spiritual-looking boy in blue nankeen, who seems to be about ten years old, to 'touch the bell;'—it was a privilege to do this;—and there he stands, that boy, whose image, more than any others, is still deeply stamped upon my mind, as I then saw him and loved him, I knew not why, and thought him so angelic and remarkable—feeling towards him more than a boy's emotion, as if a new spring of brotherly affection had suddenly broken loose in my heart. There is no indication of turbulence and disquiet about him ; but with a happy combination of energy and gentleness, how truly is he the father of the man! He has touched the bell, and while he takes his seat among his fellows, he little dreams that in after times he will strike a different note."

THE YOUNG PREACHER.

Mr. Charles T. Congdon, a veteran American journalist, in a series of papers in the New York "Tribune" in 1879, entitled "Reminiscences of a Journalist," gives some recollections of Emerson before he had abandoned his ministerial connection with the Unitarian body :—"It is curious that I should first have heard the lovable voice of Ralph Waldo Emerson, when he was the Rev. Waldo Emerson. One day there came into our pulpit the most gracious of mortals, with a face all benignity, who gave out the first hymn and made the first prayer as an angel might have read and prayed. Our choir was a pretty good one, but its best was coarse and discordant after Emerson's voice. I remember of the sermon only that it had an indefinite charm of simplicity, quaintness, and wisdom, with occasional illustrations from nature, which were about the most delicate and dainty things of the kind which I had ever heard. I could understand them, if not the fresh philosophical novelty of the discourse. Mr. Emerson preached for us for a good many Sundays, lodging in the home of a Quaker lady, just below ours. Seated at my own door, I saw him often go by, and once in the exuberance of my childish admiration I ventured to nod to him and to say 'Good morning!' To my astonishment, he also nodded and smilingly said 'Good morning!' and that is all the conversation I ever had with the sage of Concord—not enough, decidedly, for a reminiscent volume about him after he has left a world, which he has made wiser and happier. He gave us afterward two lectures based upon his travels abroad, and was at a great deal of trouble to hang up prints, by way of illustration. There was a picture of the tribune in the Uffizi Gallery in Florence, painted by one of our townsmen, and I recall Mr. Emerson's great anxiety that it should have a good light, and his lamentation when a good light was found to be impossible. The lectures themselves were so fine—enchanting we found them—that I have hungered to see them in print, and have thought of the evenings upon which they were delivered as 'true Arabian nights.'"

ORATION BEFORE THE PHI-BETA-KAPPA SOCIETY, CAMBRIDGE, IN 1837.

At page 11 of the "Memoir," allusion is made to the immense influence on the youthful mind of New England, produced by the oration before the Phi-Beta-Kappa Society, at Cambridge, on August 31, 1837. Alcott, who was present, says of it:—" I believe that was the first adequate statement of the new views that really attracted general attention. I had the good fortune to hear that address; and I shall not forget the delight with which I heard it, nor the mixed confusion, consternation, surprise, and wonder with which the audience listened to it." Lowell, who also heard it, says the delivery of this lecture "was an event without any former parallel in our literary annals, a scene to be always treasured in the memory for its picturesqueness and its inspiration. What crowded and breathless aisles, what windows clustering with eager heads, what enthusiasm of approval, what silence of foregone dissent!"

His Home and Friends.

George William Curtis, an accomplished author and orator, who at one time lived at Concord, thus spoke of Emerson's home:—" It is always morning within these doors. If you have nothing to say, if you are really not an envoy from some kingdom or colony of thought, and cannot cast a gem upon the heaped pile, you had better pass by upon the other side. For it is the peculiarity of Emerson's mind to be ever on the alert. He eats no lotus, but for ever quaffs the waters which engender immortal thirst. . . . The fame of the philosopher attracts admiring friends and enthusiasts from every quarter, and the scholarly grace and urbane hospitality of the gentleman send them charmed away. . . . It is not hazardous to say that the greatest questions of our day and of all days have been nowhere more amply discussed, with more poetic insight or more profound conviction, than in the comely square white house upon the edge of the Lexington turnpike. . . . 'I chide society, I embrace solitude,' he says, 'and yet I am not so ungrateful as not to see the wise, the lovely, and the noble-minded, as from time to time they pass my gate.' It is not difficult to understand his fondness for the spot. He has always been familiar with it, always more or less a resident of the village. Born in Boston upon the spot where Channery Place Church now stands, part of his youth was passed in the Old Manse, which was built by his grandfather, and in which his father was born; and there he wrote 'Nature.' The imagination of the man who roams the solitary pastures of Concord, or floats dreaming down its river, will easily see its landscape upon Emerson's page. If there be something oriental in his philosophy and tropical in his imagination, they have yet a strong flavour of his mother earth—the underived sweetness of the open Concord sky, and the spacious breadth of the Concord horizon." In 1845 there was something like a club formed, whose members met in Emerson's library on Monday evenings. This library is described by Mr. Curtis. "It is a simple square room, not walled with books like the den of a literary grub, nor merely elegant like the ornamental retreat of a dilettante. The books are arranged upon plain shelves, not in architectural bookcases, and the room is hung with a few choice engravings of the greatest men. There was a fair copy of Michael Angelo's 'Fates,' which, properly enough, imparted that grave serenity to the ornament of the room which is always apparent in what is written there." Here the scholars met at their symposium. "Plato" (Alcott) "was perpetually putting apples of gold in pictures of silver; for such was the rich ore of his thoughts, coined by the deep melody of his voice. Orson" (Thoreau) "charmed us with the secrets won from his interviews with Pan in the Walden woods—while Emerson, with the zeal of an engineer trying to dam wild waters, sought to bind the wide-flying embroidery of discourse into a web of clear sweet sense. . . . Miles Coverdale" (Hawthorne), "a statue of night and silence, sat, a little removed, under a portrait of Dante, gazing imperturbably upon the group; and as he sat in the shadow, his dark hair and eyes and suit of sable made him, in that society, the black thread of mystery he weaves into his stories."

Mr. Alcott once wrote thus of Emerson :—" Fortunate the visitor who is admitted of a morning for the high discourse, or permitted to join the poet in his afternoon walks to Walden, the Cliffs, or elsewhere,—hours to be remembered as unlike any others in the calendar of experiences. Shall I describe them as sallies oftenest into the cloudlands,—into scenes and intimacies ever new, none the less novel nor remote than when first experienced ?—interviews, however, bringing their own trail of perplexing thoughts,—costing some days' duties, several nights' sleep oftentimes, to restore one to his place and poise. Certainly safer not to venture without the sure credentials, unless one will have his pretensions pricked, his conceits reduced in their vague dimensions. But to the modest, the ingenuous, the gifted—welcome! nor can any bearing be more poetic and polite to all such,—to youth and accomplished women especially. His is a faith approaching to superstition concerning admirable persons, the rumour of excellence of any sort being like the arrival of a new gift to mankind, and he the first to proffer his recognition and hope." Concord was for many years a kind of Mecca to which many a devout and faithful pilgrim resorted. "Young visionaries (in the words of Hawthorne), to whom just so much of insight had been imparted as to make life all a labyrinth around them, came to seek the clew that should lead them out of their self-involved bewilderment. Grey-headed theorists—whose systems, at first air, had imprisoned them in an iron frame-work—travelled painfully to his door, not to ask deliverance, but to invite the free spirit into their own thraldom. People that had lighted on a new thought, or a thought that they fancied new, came to Emerson, as the finder of a glittering gem hastens to a lapidary to ascertain its value. For myself, there had been epochs in my life when it, too, might have asked of this prophet the master-word that should solve me the riddle of the universe; but now, being happy, I felt as if there were no question to be put, and therefore admired Emerson as a poet of deep beauty and austere tenderness, but sought nothing from him as a philosopher."

A writer in the "Chicago Times," a few years ago, thus wrote from his own knowledge of Emerson:—" Although one of the severest of students and most abstract of philosophers, he always emerges from his library to the family circle with evident satisfaction. Notwithstanding a certain gravity of manner, he is full of geniality and *bonhomie*, and is never more eloquent and charming than when away from his books and manuscripts. He is very fond of children and young people; loves to talk and walk with them, and listens to them as if they were revealing the oracles of the gods. No man in Concord is more popular or accessible than he. He is fully in sympathy with the old town; he reveres and honours it, and says he would not exchange it for New York, Athens, Rome, or Paris. To get a clear and adequate conception of Emerson, one must see him at home, in undress, so to speak, if he may be considered as ever in uniform, who is the soul of simplicity and sincerity. He is the kindest of husbands, the most considerate of fathers. It is related of him that when any thought strikes him, when any suggestion occurs, or any pat quotation is recalled, he invariably stops the thing he is doing and jots down the thought or suggestion for future use or reference. Even in the middle of the night he observes this habit, knowing that a good thing may be lost forever unless recorded. Before his second wife got used to his ways, she would ask him, when he arose to strike a light, 'Are you ill, husband?' 'No, my dear,' he would reply, 'only an idea.' . . . Nobody has ever seen him out of temper, or even ruffled. He is the embodiment of calm courtesy, of placid refinement—the very reverse of the supremely nervous, irritable being an author is believed to be, and often is, in truth."

Miss Frederika Bremer's Visit to Emerson.

In her "Homes of the New World," Miss Bremer gives the following account of a visit she paid to Mr. Emerson at his home in Concord, in 1849:—"During the four days that I remained in Emerson's house I had a real enjoyment in the study of this strong, noble, eagle-like nature. Any near approximation was, as it were, imperfect, because our characters and views are fundamentally dissimilar, and that secret antagonism which exists in me towards him, spite of my admiration, would at times awake, and this easily called forth his icy-alp nature, repulsive and chilly. But this is not the original nature of the man—he does not rightly thrive in it, and he gladly throws it off if he can, and is much happier, as one can see, in a mild and sunny atmosphere where the natural beauty of his being may breathe freely and expand into blossom, touched by that of others as by a living breeze.

"I enjoyed the contemplation of him in his demeanour, his expression, his mode of talking, and his every-day life, as I enjoy contemplating the calm flow of a river bearing along and between flowery shores large and small vessels, as I love to see the eagle circling in the clouds, resting upon them and its pinions. In this calm elevation Emerson allows nothing to reach him, neither great nor small, neither prosperity nor adversity.

"Pantheistic as Emerson is in his Philosophy, in the moral view with which he regards the world and life, he is in a high degree pure, noble, and severe, demanding as much from himself as he demands from others. His words are severe, his judgment often keen and merciless, but his demeanour is alike noble and pleasing and his voice beautiful.

"One may quarrel with Emerson's thoughts, with his judgment, but not with himself. That which struck me most, as distinguishing him from most other human beings, is nobility. He is a born nobleman. I have seen before two other men born with this stamp upon them—his excellency

W———r, in Sweden, and ——— is the second, Emerson the third which has it, and perhaps in a yet higher degree; and added thereto that deep intonation of voice, that expression so mild yet so elevated at the same time. I could not but think of Maria Lowell's words, 'If he merely mention my name, I feel myself ennobled.'

"I enjoyed Emerson's conversation, which flowed as calmly and easily as a deep and placid river. It was animating to me both when I agreed and when I dissented; there is always a something important in what he says, and he listens well and comprehends and replies well also. But whether it was the weariness of the spirit or whether a feeling of esteem for his peace and freedom, I know not, but I did not invite his conversation. When it came it was good, when it did not come it was good also, especially if he were in the room. His presence was agreeable to me. He was amiable in his attention to me and in his mode of entertaining me as a stranger and guest in his house.

"This is what I wished to say to Emerson, what I endeavoured to say, but I know not how I did it. I cannot usually express myself either easily or successfully until I become warm and get beyond or through the first thoughts; and Emerson's cool, and as it were circumspect, manner prevented me from getting into my own natural region. I like to be with him, but when with him I am never fully myself. I do not believe that I now expressed myself intelligibly to him. He listened calmly, and said nothing decidedly against it, nor yet seemed inclined to give his views as definite. He seemed to me principally to be opposed to blind or hypocritical faith. 'I do not wish,' said he, 'that people should pretend to know or to believe more than they really do know and believe. The resurrection, the continuance of our being, is granted,' said he also; 'we carry the pledges of this in our own breast. I maintain merely that we cannot say in what form or in what manner our existence will be continued.' If my conversation with Emerson did not lead to anything very satisfactory, it led, nevertheless, to my still more firm conviction of his nobility and love of truth. He is faithful to the law in his own breast, and speaks out the truth which he inwardly recognises. He does right. By this means he will prepare the way for a more true comprehension of religion and of life. For when once this keen glance, seeing into the innermost of everything, once becomes aware of the concealed human form in the tree of life—like Napoleon's in the tree of St. Helena—then will he teach others to see it too, will point it out by such strong, new, and glorious words that a fresh light will spring up before many, and people will believe because they see."

The "Brook Farm Community" Experiment.

A friend of Emerson gives the following account of this singular movement, which Hawthorne with his inimitable and weird pencil has immortalized in that saddest of romances, "The Blithedale Romance:"—"It was indescribably ludicrous to observe reverend doctors and other dons coming out to gaze upon the extraordinary spectacle, and going about as dainty ladies hold their skirts and daintily step from stone to stone in a muddy street, lest they be soiled. The dons seemed to doubt whether the mere contact had not smirched them. But, droll in itself, it was a thousandfold droller when Theodore Parker came through the woods and described it. With his head set low upon his gladiatorial shoulders, and his nasal voice in subtle and exquisite mimicry reproducing what was truly laughable, yet all with infinite *bonhomie* and with a genuine superiority to small malice, he was as humorous as he was learned, and as excellent a man as he was noble and fervent and humane a preacher. On Sundays a party always went from the Farm to Mr. Parker's little country church. He was there exactly what he was afterwards when he preached to thousands of eager people in the Boston Music Hall; the same plain, simple, rustic, racy man. His congregation were his personal friends. They loved him and admired him and were proud of him; and his geniality and tender sympathy, his ample knowledge of things as well as of books, his jovial manliness and sturdy independence, drew to him all ages and sexes and conditions. The society at Brook Farm was composed of every kind of person. There were the ripest scholars, men and women of the most æsthetic culture and accomplishment, young farmers, seamstresses, mechanics, preachers—the industrious, the lazy, the conceited, the sentimental. But they were associated in such a spirit and under such conditions that, with some extravagance, the best of everybody appeared, and there was a kind of *esprit de corps*, at least in the earlier or golden age of the colony. There was plenty of steady, essential hard work; for the founding of an earthly Paradise upon a rough New England farm is no pastime. But with the best intention, and much practical knowledge and industry and devotion, there was in the nature of the case an inevitable lack of method, and the economical failure was almost a foregone conclusion. But there were never such witty potato patches and such sparkling corn-fields before or since. The weeds were scratched out of the ground to the music of Tennyson or Browning, and the nooning was an hour as gay and bright as any brilliant midnight at Ambrose's. But in the midst of all was one figure, the practical farmer, an honest neighbour who was not drawn to the enterprise by any spiritual attraction, but was hired at good wages to superintend the work, and who always seemed to be regarding the whole affair with the most good-natured wonder as a prodigious masquerade. Indeed, the description which Hawthorne gives of him at a real masquerade of the farmers in the woods depicts his attitude toward Brook Farm itself: 'And apart, with a shrewd Yankee observation of the scene, stands our friend Orange, a thick-set, sturdy figure, enjoying the fun well enough, yet rather laughing with a perception of its nonsensicalness than at all entering into the spirit of the thing.' That, indeed, was very much the attitude of Hawthorne himself toward Brook Farm and many other aspects of human life. But beneath all the glancing colours, the lights and shadows of its surface, it was a simple, honest, practical effort for wiser forms of life than those in which we find ourselves. The criticism of science, the sneer of literature, the complaint of experience, is that man is a miserably half-developed being, the proof of which is the condition of human society, in which the few enjoy and the many toil. But the enjoyment cloys and disappoints, and the very want of labour poisons the enjoyment. Man is made body and soul. The health of each requires reasonable exercise. If every man did his share of the muscular work of the world, no other man would be overwhelmed by it. The man who does not work imposes harder toil upon him who does. Thereby the first steals from the last the opportunity of mental culture, and at last we reach a world of pariahs and patricians, with all the inconceivable sorrow and suffering that surround us. Bound fast by the brazen age, we can see that the way back to the age of gold lies through justice, which will substitute co-operation for competition. . . . The spirit that was concentrated at Brook Farm is diffused, but it is not lost. As an organised effort, after many downward changes, it failed; but those who remember the Hive, the Eyrie, the Cottage—when Margaret Fuller came and talked, radiant with bright humour; when Emerson and Parker and Hedge joined the circle for a night or a day; when those who may not be publicly named brought beauty and wit and social sympathy to the feast; when the practical possibilities of life seemed fairer, and life and character were touched ineffaceably with good influence—cherish a pleasant vision which no fate can harm, and remember with ceaseless gratitude the blithe days at Brook Farm."

Mr. Alcott and his Daughters.

The following account of the venerable Mr. Bronson Alcott, Emerson's life-long friend, still living, in his eighty-third year, will be read with interest. His name is inseparably associated with that of his distinguished fellow-townsman. It is from a paper in the New York "Home Journal," entitled "Literati at Concord," November, 1874 :—

"Not far from Mr. Emerson's hemlock grove—writes a pilgrim of the Inter-Ocean—is the picturesque home of the Alcotts. It is the queerest little cottage in the world. It stands at the foot of the hill which the British soldiers crossed the morning, nearly a hundred years ago, when they marched up from Lexington. The house is a dull brown colour, with peaked roof and many a gable end, in one of which, hooded by the jutting roof and festooned by some airy sprays of woodbine, is the window whence 'Aunt Joe' looks out on the sunny meadows. On each side of the front walk there is a huge elm with rustic seat built around its roots, and among the branches tame squirrels hold high revelry. Yonder a hammock swings under some apple trees, and around the whole runs a rustic fence, built by Mr. Alcott himself. It is made entirely of pine boughs, knotted, gnarled, and twisted into every conceivable shape. No two pieces are alike ; the gates are wonderful, and they alone would make credible the story that he spent years collecting the branches.

"Mr. Alcott, the 'Orphic Alcott,' as Curtis calls him, is one of the Concord philosophers, and has his 'ism,' of course. Vegetables and conversation are his *forte*, and he reared his family on a diet of both, apparently with great success, judging from appearances. He ate weeds and talked and built summer-houses, whose chief use was to be targets for George William Curtis' wit. Once he kept a young ladies' school in Boston, where books were discarded and teaching done entirely by conversation. He was also a member of those extraordinary assemblages, practicable in Boston alone, over which Margaret Fuller presided, and it must have been a rare sight to see how these two inexhaustible talkers managed to tolerate each other. For it is said that Mr. Alcott's conversations are very much like the Irishman's treaty—the reciprocity is all on one side ; or, as a Western host described him once in his invitations to some friends, 'Come up this evening. I have a philosopher on tap.'

"It is all well enough to joke about Mr. Alcott till you see him. Then to come face to face with this white-haired, benign, gracious old man, makes levity seem irreverent. He is over six feet tall, but a good deal stooped. His long, grey hair falls scantily around a face beautified by the placidity and dignity of old age ; he is a perfect counterpart of the pictures of venerable *curés* one sees in French story books. His manners are very simple and unaffected, and it is his great delight to gather some of his daughters' young friends in his cosy, crimson-lined study and chat with them. Mr. Emerson esteems him highly, but his books seem to be less appreciated by his own people than they are abroad, a fate common to prophets if not philosophers. His most valuable work is a journal faithfully kept for fifty years, carefully bound, indexed, and with letters and other valuable papers ranged on his library shelves. This taste for minute detail, his orderly arrangement, his distinguished associates, and the number of years covered by the record will make these volumes priceless to historians or biographers. If in Emerson's study perpetual twilight reigns, in Alcott's it is always noon. The sun shines in it all day long, the great fireplace roars, and the warm crimson hangings temper the sunlight and reflect the firelight. Quaint mottoes and pictures hang on the walls. The most noticeable picture is a photograph of Carlyle. It is what is called a 'Cameron photograph.' An English woman of rank takes these photographs of distinguished men just for her own amusement. The camera is set out of focus, the heads nearly life-size, and the general effect is singular—interesting, if nothing else. All you can see against a black background is the indistinct outlines of a shaggy white head and beard and sharp features. With all deference to Mr. Carlyle, we must say that he looks like an old beggar.

"Miss May Alcott, a fine-looking, stylish woman, is an artist whom the critic of critics, Ruskin, has declared to be the only successful copyist of Turner. She surely has one attribute not usually allied to her profession—the most generous interest in other artists—not only by word of mouth, but with substantial endeavour. She brought home with her several English water colours, for whose artists she is trying to find American patrons. She herself paints in oil and water colours, and sketches in crayons, charcoal, sepia, ink, and pencil, and is one of the most popular Boston teachers. Her studio at home, a most cobwebby, disorderly, fascinating little den, is frescoed with profiles of her acquaintances—that is the toll cheerfully paid by her visitors—they must be drawn on the wall. She is known to the general reading public through her illustrations of 'Little Women,' in which she fell far short of her usual ability. She and Louisa planned subsequently a charming little book called 'Concord Sketches,' which it is a great pity was never made public. Beside painting, Miss May models in clay sometimes. A head of Mercury and all sorts of pretty little sketches from her hands adorn her home, which is made a still sunnier remembrance to all visitors by her brightness and cordiality. [This lady died some years ago.]

"Louisa Alcott, the elder of the two, the darling of all American nurseries, is something of an invalid. She is amiable and interesting, and, like her sister, sociable, unless you unluckily approach her in her character of author, and then the porcupine bristles. There is no favour to be curried with her or Gail Hamilton by talking 'shop.' 'Little Women' is drawn chiefly from Miss Alcott's own home life. Amy the golden-haired, is May, Hemmie and Demmie are her two little nephews, Mr. and Mrs. Marsh her father and mother; she herself is Jo, of course. When the book was first published, children used to come by the dozen from all parts of the country to see 'Jo.' To the calls of these little pilgrims she always presented herself cheerfully, though she used to be infinitely amused at the unmistakable disappointment of her young admirers when they saw this delicate, practical-looking lady, slightly stooped, for their rollicking, romping, nimble Jo. Miss Alcott struck a rich vein of popularity and more substantial reward in her juvenile books, though she herself considers 'Hospital Sketches' the best of her writings.

"Some four or five years ago she went into a Boston bookstore to leave an order, which the clerk told her could not be attended to, 'because,' said he, not knowing to whom he spoke, 'we shall be busy all day packing books for a Western firm. Two weeks ago we sent ten thousand copies of "Little Women" out there, and to-day comes an order for twenty thousand more.' As soon as they got out of the store her companion turned to her with some congratulatory expression.

"'Ah!' said Miss Alcott, drawing a long breath, 'I have waited fifteen years for this day.'

"Mrs. Alcott is a beautiful old lady, herself something of a writer, or, as one of her daughters lovingly says, 'the brightest one of the family.'"

"Monday Conversations" at Concord.

A writer in the "Boston Journal" (April 27, 1872,) gives an account of Emerson's "Monday Conversations" and "Literary Meetings" at the Mechanics' Hall, Concord :—" A venerable gentleman, well preserved, serene and elegant in manner, takes his seat upon the platform of a cosy and comfortable hall, at three o'clock on a Monday afternoon, when the rush and roar of business in practical Boston is at its height, and, gently arranging his papers before him, looks calmly around him upon the large audience gathered to hear him. It is the *causerie* which he has undertaken—the familiar and delicate enunciation of his ideas in the form invented by our sprightly yet thoughtful French friends—and the ladies throng to hear him in greater numbers even than when he appears in the attitude of the lecturer. A red curtain hangs behind him, setting off in sharp relief the keen and noble outline of his features—the head thrown forward with the poise of daring assertion—and the face now animated with all the warmth and enthusiasm of a genuine poetic admiration, now saddened and reserved with the diffidence of the habitual student and the man of reverie. Side-lights from each wing of the stage throw a sharp light upon the ample manuscript on the reading-desk, for the philosopher and poet is now rapidly nearing seventy years of age, and the fatigues of the lecture-room are easier felt than thirty years ago. Yet the same consummate magnetism lingers around and upon every word and phrase; there is the same thrilling earnestness of antithesis, the same delight and gloating over poetry and excellence of expression, as of old. There is no other man in America who can, by the mere force of what he says, enthrall and dominate an audience. Breathless attention is given, although now and then his voice falls away so that those seated farthest off have to strain every nerve to catch the words. The grand condensation, the unfaltering and almost cynical brevity of expression are at first startling and vexatious; but presently one yields to the charm, and finds his mind in the proper assenting mood. The conversations attract more women than men, but they are of the more intellectual and reflective class of our New England women, who find in the intensity and wonderful precision of Mr. Emerson's mind something inexpressibly pleasing. Nor are they blind worshippers merely at a shrine before which they kneel in wonder; but the large majority appreciate and enjoy to the uttermost the continual, unresting surging of thought thrust upon them. . . . Mr. Emerson is greeted by a class of people who are rarely seen together on any other public occasion in Boston. Aside from the large number of professed admirers and disciples, and the literati, who are present each time that he speaks or reads in Boston or vicinity, the men who go to hear him are mainly of the desire-to-be-dazzled-and-shocked order, who seem disagreeably surprised when they do comprehend what he says. Mr. Emerson's terse and vivid sentences cling in the memory, and will not be effaced. The *causerie* of yesterday afternoon gave an hundred ideas upon poetry, and the relations of nature to man, which will be henceforth grafted inseparably upon the common mind. The emphatic New Englander listens, incredulously at first, but finishes by saying, 'That's so!' Ideals and heretofore far-remote abstractions are brought down to the sphere of daily life—admirably illustrated—made plain, and tethered where even the humblest can appreciate them as realities. And in all cases it seems to the listener as if the phrases uttered were sculptured in the thought of the speaker—as if they had been so from the beginning, and could never be otherwise."

EMERSON AND HIS DAUGHTER.

A correspondent of the "Cincinnati Commercial," giving an account of a lecture delivered at Cincinnati in July, 1876, thus speaks of the beautiful relation between Mr. Emerson and his daughter:—"Into the Congressional library walked Emerson, one of the immortals, and smiled his celestial smile, as if two such things as mercury and the thermometer were not. His daughter Ellen by his side, and as she is the incarnation of common sense, she also was sublimely indifferent to the weather. When this rare spirit (far be the day) passes forever from mortal sight we shall hear more from this daughter Ellen. For she, in all likelihood, will be the executor of his papers and the delineator of that deep, still, inward life. It is memorable that the men who have achieved the most in letters and in science have always had a woman standing close beside them within the veil, as Carl Schurz says in homely phrase: 'Handing them the bricks while they build,' and holding up their hands when they were weary. It has just come to light how much Sir William Herschel owed to the tender and tireless sister who, through a lifetime of nights, stood by his side while others slept; who polished till her hands grew numb the mirrors which were to reflect back for him immensity; who had no ambition in life but to be his servant; who underrated her own achievements that she might exalt his, and, as her clear vision swept the paths of the spheres, shrank from her own discoveries of worlds, lest it might prove a shadow on his fame. So the great American seer has a woman walking close by his side, taking the very thoughts from his mind and translating them for the world, and this woman is his daughter."

Literary Opinions.

A few years ago, an English literary gentleman visited Emerson at his home in Concord, and brought away many of his opinions on literary and other subjects. A few of these are here recorded:—"Wordsworth's ode on Immortality touches the high water mark of modern literature. . . . Walter Savage Landor will always be read by the select few. Matthew Arnold is growing too diffusive. His 'sweetness and light' have become as heavy as lead with too much repetition. He liked Arnold's critical essays very much, but was not partial to his poetry. Sainte-Beuve he considered the great French writer. He said 'I don't meddle with Auguste Comte,' in reply to the question whether he was interested in the positive philosophy. . . . 'Thoreau was a true genius, and so great was his mastery of the phenomena of nature that it would need another Linnæus, as well as a poet, properly to edit his writings.' . . . Of Buckle he spoke with admiration, comparing his erudition with Gibbon's fulness of learning, and cited his chapters on France in particular as a splendid contribution to history. . . . Carlyle being mentioned, Emerson defended him from Margaret Fuller's criticism in her letters, and said that 'Carlyle purposely made exaggerated statements, merely to astonish his listeners. His attitude toward America during our war was unfortunate, but no more than could be expected.'" Mr. Emerson's visitor records what Carlyle is reported to have said regarding a distinguished English poet of the "fleshly school," but the *pronunciamento* is so scathing and unprintable that I dare not venture to give it currency.

The "School of Philosophy" at Concord, 1880.

The Concord Correspondent of the "Chicago Tribune" (September, 1880) gives the following sketch of Emerson at the age of seventy-seven:—"An old man with large eyes, prominent nose, and awkward carriage, may often be seen shyly stealing into the 'School of Philosophy,' just after the beginning of the lecture. Passing through the aisle on tiptoe, he seats himself in a huge ear-lap chair at the left of the platform. The lips of the Sphinx are sealed, and their peaceful expression and the far-away look in the eyes would seem to indicate that the discussion going on has not sufficient interest to draw him from the calm joy of reverie. But the way in which he leans forward now and then to catch the tones of an indistinct speaker, and the promptitude with which certain little red spots appear on his cheeks whenever a personal allusion or quotation is made, show that, after all, he is listening with respectful attention. Emerson has a noble propensity to overrate the works of his contemporaries. He has such a sublime faith that the coming man will eventually arrive, that he is always on the look out for him, and finds his John the Baptists in eccentric Thoreau and uncouth Whitman, in whom so many see only insanity. And especially does his unaffected humility place an exaggerated estimate upon the works and words of his personal friends. Thoreau was an original genius, and his mother used to say: 'Why, how much Mr. Emerson talks like Henry!' Some people are unkind enough to say that the boot was squarely on the other foot, and that Thoreau was only a parody of his great friend. While such statements are grossly unjust, it remains true that the fame of the poet naturalist owes much to the friendship of Emerson, who not only gave him warm encouragement and unstinted praise, but made himself pecuniarily responsible in order that 'Walden' and 'The Week' might be given to the world by a hesitating publisher. Emerson's house was thrown open last Sunday evening, and parlour and study and hall were filled with friends from the town and the School of Philosophy. Mr. and Mrs. Emerson (whose quaint, sweet face and simple, old-fashioned attire suggested to one lady that 'She might have just stepped off the *Mayflower*') bustled around, shaking hands and arranging chairs for the guests. Then Mr. Emerson rapped upon a door-jamb and said: 'Some of our friends have something to say to us, and we shall be glad to have them begin.' Mr. Channing, Mr. Alcott, Miss Peabody and Professor Harris did most of the talking. Mrs. Emerson made a single remark, but the host took no part whatever. The seventy-seventh birthday of Mr. Emerson occurred recently. He feels the weight of years, and though he walks about briskly, his memory is failing, and he is often thrown into pathetic confusion by his treacherous faculty. It seems very difficult for him to grasp a new name. Joseph Cook called upon him just after Moody and Sankey had been in Boston, and he inquired of his visitor if he had been attending the 'Mosely and Sukey meetings!' He never appeared in public without his faithful maiden daughter Ellen, who has the face of a saint and the garb of a Quakeress. She has charge of his manuscripts, and when asked, a few days ago, what lecture her father proposed to read before the school, replied that 'she had not decided.' She intimated, furthermore, that she might put a veto on his lecturing at all."

A Touching Conversation with him in 1881.

A visitor at Concord, in August, 1881, records the following touching conversation with Emerson. "Just on the outskirts of the village, a little way back from the street, stands the old-fashioned country-seat which is sacred as being the home of the Jove of the Concord Immortals, Emerson. Mr. Emerson himself came to the door to greet me with a still active step, and with his placid, inscrutable countenance unchanged in the eight years since I had seen him last. A vein of sadness ran through his striking words as we conversed, which now and then deepened into indescribable pathos as he spoke of himself:—

"'I am visiting the Summer School, and called to pay my respects to you,' I said.

"'I thank you,' he replied, and a slight difficulty in articulation was noticeable as he spoke. 'I am glad to see you; yet I fear I can do little. I can only disappoint those who come to see me. I find that I am losing myself, and I wander away from the matter that I have in mind.' There was little to be said, but I made some remark, and he continued:

"'I cannot say much. When I begin I lose myself. And so when my friends come to see me I run away, instead of going to meet them, that I may not make them suffer.'

"I spoke of an examining committee on which he had served at Cambridge, and his face lightened for an instant. 'Yes, yes,' he said, and made some personal enquiry of me. 'But I see no one now,' he added.

"'Your general health is good, I trust?' I asked.

"'Yes, my health is good enough,' he replied indifferently. Then he said slowly, with a wonderful pathos in his voice: 'But when one's wits begin to fail, it is time for the heavens to open and take him away.'

"He turned sadly aside, and I left him. More keenly than anyone else can do, the philosopher realises that age is casting a shadow upon his memory and slowly chilling his faculties."

Mr. Holyoake's Visit.

Mr. George Jacob Holyoake, in the latest chapter of his recent American tour in the "Co-operative News," describes a visit he paid to Emerson:—"Though tall, he is still erect, and has the bright eye and calm grace of manner we knew when he was in England long years ago. In European eyes, his position among men of letters in America is as that of Carlyle among English writers; with the added quality, as I think, of greater braveness of thought and clearness of sympathy. . . . Friends had told me that age seemed now a little to impair Mr. Emerson's memory, but I found his recollection of England accurate and full of detail. Englishmen told me with pride that in the dark days of the war, when American audiences were indignant at England, Emerson would put in his lectures some generous passage concerning this country, and raising himself erect, pronounce it in a defiant tone, as though he threw the words at his audience. More than any other writer Emerson gives me the impression of one who sees facts alive and knows their ways, and who writes nothing that is mean or poor."

Two Characteristic Anecdotes.

Some twenty years ago Emerson addressed a literary society, during Commencement, at Middlebury, Vermont, and when he ended, the President called upon a clergyman to conclude the service with prayer. Then arose a Massachusetts minister, who stepped into the pulpit Mr. Emerson had just left, and uttered a remarkable prayer, of which this was one sentence: "We beseech Thee, O Lord, to deliver us from ever hearing any more such transcendental nonsense as we have just listened to from this sacred desk." After the benediction, Mr. Emerson asked his next neighbour the name of the officiating clergyman, and when falteringly answered, with gentle simplicity remarked: "He seemed a very conscientious, plain-spoken man," and went on his peaceful way.

"Mr. Giles, the Irish essayist, told me a nice little story of Emerson, with which this chapter may conclude. We had a rich old merchant, who was a tireless talker, with whom our lecturers sometimes lodged. The good-hearted gentleman caught Mr. Giles one evening and kept him a complaisant but dreadfully weary listener, morally button-holed, so to speak, until nearly sunrise. Then, as they parted for the night, or rather for the morning, the garrulous and gratified monologist said: 'I like you, Mr. Giles; you are willing to hear what I have to say; Mr. Emerson was here the other night, after he had lectured, and he said he did not wish to hear me talk—that he had rather go to bed.' Not that the kindest of men meant to be uncivil—he merely spoke with the simplicity and directness of a Greek philosopher."

The Latest Glimpses of Emerson in his Home.

One of the latest glimpses we have of Emerson, in his home surroundings, is from the journal of Walt Whitman, the American poet, who paid a visit to Concord in the Autumn of last year (1881). He dined with Emerson and his family, and spent several hours on two successive days in their company. The following sentences I cull from Whitman's journal now before me:—

"*Camden, N. J., Dec. 1, 1881.*—During my last three or four months' jaunt to Boston and through New England, I spent such good days at Concord, and with Emerson, seeing him under such propitious circumstances, in the calm, peaceful, but most radiant, twilight of his old age (nothing in the height of his literary action and expression so becoming and impressive), that I must give a few impromptu notes of it all. So I devote this cluster entirely to the man, to the place, the past, and all leading up to, and forming, that memorable and peculiar Personality, now near his 80th year—as I have just seen him there, in his home,—silent, sunny, surrounded by a beautiful family."

"*Concord, Mass., Sept. 17.*—Never had I a better piece of better luck befall me: a long and blessed evening with Emerson, in a way I couldn't have wished better or different. For nearly two hours he has been placidly sitting where I could see his face in the best light near me. Mrs. S.'s back parlour well fill'd with people, neighbours, many fresh and charming faces, women, mostly young, but some old. My friend A. B. Alcott and his daughter Louisa were there early. A good deal of talk, the subject Henry Thoreau—some new glints of his life and fortunes, with letters to and from him—one of the best by Margaret Fuller, others by Horace Greeley, W. H. Channing, etc.—one from Thoreau himself, most quaint and interesting. My seat and the relative arrangement were such that, without being rude or anything of the kind, I could just look squarely at E., which I did a good part of the two hours. On entering he had spoken very briefly, easily and politely to several of the company, then settled himself in his chair, a trifle pushed back, and, though a listener and apparently an alert one, remained silent through the whole talk and discussion. And so, there Emerson sat, and I looking at him. A good colour in his face, eyes clear, with the well-known expression of sweetness, and the old clear-peering aspect quite the same."

"*Next Day.*—Several hours at E.'s house, and dinner there. An old familiar house (he has been in it thirty-five years), with the surrounding furnishment, roominess, and plain elegance and fulness, signifying democratic ease, sufficient opulence, and an admirable old-fashioned simplicity—modern luxury, with its mere sumptuousness and affectation, either touched lightly upon, or ignored altogether, Of course the best of the present occasion (Sunday, September 18th, 1881) was the sight of E. himself. As just said, a healthy colour in the cheeks, and good light in the eyes, cheery expression, and just the amount of talking that best suited, namely, a word or short phrase only where needed, and almost always with a smile. Besides Emerson himself, Mrs. E., with their daughter Ellen, the son Edward and his wife, with my friend F. S. and Mrs. S., and others, relatives and intimates. Mrs. Emerson, resuming the subject of the evening before (I sat next to her), gave me further and fuller information about Thoreau, who years ago, during Mr. E.'s absence in Europe in 1848, had lived for some time in the family, by invitation.

"Let me conclude by the thought, after all the rest is said, that most impresses me about Emerson. Amid the utter delirium-disease called book-making, its feverish cohorts filling our world with every form of dislocation, morbidity, and special type of anemia or exceptionalism (with the propelling idea of getting the most possible money, first of all), how comforting to know of an author who has, through a long life, and in spirit, written as honestly, spontaneously, and innocently, as the sun shines or the wheat grows—the truest, sanest, most moral, sweetest literary man on record—unsoiled by pecuniary or any other warp—ever teaching the law within—ever loyally outcropping his own self only—his own poetic and devout soul! If there be a Spirit above that looks down and scans authors, here is one at least in whom it might be well pleased."

EMERSON AND CARLYLE.
From "A Fable for Critics."
By JAMES RUSSELL LOWELL.

There comes Emerson first, whose rich words, every one,
Are like gold nails in temples to hang trophies on. . . .
A Greek head on right Yankee shoulders, whose range
Has Olympus for one pole, for t'other the Exchange;
He seems, to my thinking (although I'm afraid
The comparison must, long ere this, have been made),
A Plotinus-Montaigne, where the Egyptian's gold mist
And the Gascon's shrewd wit cheek-by-jowl co-exist;
All admire, and yet scarcely six converts he's got
To I don't (nor they either) exactly know what;
For though he builds glorious temples, 'tis odd
He leaves never a doorway to get in a god.

'Tis refreshing to old-fashioned people like me
To meet such a primitive Pagan as he,
In whose mind all creation is duly respected
As parts of himself, just a little projected;
And who's willing to worship the stars and the sun,
A convert to—nothing but Emerson.
So perfect a balance there is in his head,
That he talks of things sometimes as if they were dead;
Life, nature, love, God, and affairs of that sort,
He looks at as merely ideas; in short,
As if they were fossils stuck round in a cabinet,
Of such vast extent that our earth's a mere dab in it;
Composed just as he is inclined to conjecture her—
Namely, one part pure earth, ninety-nine parts pure lecturer;
You are filled with delight at his clear demonstration,
Each figure, word, gesture just fits the occasion,
With the quiet precision of science he'll sort 'em,
But you can't help suspecting the whole a *post mortem.*
There are persons, mole-blind to the soul's make and style,
Who insist on a likeness 'twixt him and Carlyle;
To compare him with Plato would be vastly fairer,
Carlyle's the more burly, but E. is the rarer;
He sees fewer objects, but clearlier, truelier—
If C.'s an original, E.'s more peculiar;
That he's more of a man you might say of the one,
Of the other he's more of an Emerson;
C.'s the Titan, as shaggy of mind as of limb –
E., the clear-eyed Olympian, rapid and slim;
The one's two-thirds Norseman, the other half Greek,
Where the one's most abounding, the other's to seek;
C.'s generals require to be seen in the mass,—
E.'s specialities gain if enlarged by the glass;
C. gives nature and God his own fits of the blues,
And rims common-sense things with mystical hues,—
E. sits in a mystery calm and intense,
And looks coolly around him with sharp common-sense;
C. shews you how every-day matters unite
With the dim transdiurnal recesses of night,—
While E. in a plain, præternatural way,
Makes mysteries matters of mere every day.
E. is rather like Flaxman, lines straight and severe,
And a colourless outline, but full, round, and clear;—
To the men he thinks worthy he frankly accords
The design of a white marble statue in words.
C. labours to get at the centre, and then
Take a reckoning from there of his actions and men;
E. calmly assumes the said centre as granted,
And, given himself, has whatever is wanted.

Emerson's Speech in Manchester.

[This speech (referred to in "Memoir," p. 14) was delivered at a soirée, held under the auspices of the Manchester Athenæum, at the Free Trade Hall, in November, 1847, under the presidency of Sir A. Alison, the historian, and at which Richard Cobden and other political leaders were present. Of this meeting Mr. Emerson says in his "English Traits:" "A few days after my arrival in Manchester, in November, 1847, the Manchester Athenæum gave its annual banquet in the Free Trade Hall. With other guests, I was invited to be present, and to address the company. In looking over recently a newspaper report of my remarks, I inclined to reprint it as fully expressing the feeling with which I entered England, and which agrees well enough with the more deliberate results of better acquaintance recorded in the foregoing pages. Sir Archibald Alison, the historian, presided, and opened the meeting with a speech. He was followed by Mr. Cobden, Lord Brackley, and others, among whom was Mr. Cruikshank, one of the contributors to 'Punch.' Mr. Dickens's letter of apology for his absence was read. Mr. Jerrold, who had been announced, did not appear."]

Mr. Chairman and gentlemen,—It is pleasant to me to meet this great and brilliant company, and doubly pleasant to see the faces of so many distinguished persons on this platform. But I have known all these persons already. When I was at home they were as near to me as they are to you. The arguments of the League and its leader are known to all the friends of trade. The gaieties and genius, the political, the social, the parietal wit of "Punch" go duly every fortnight to every boy and girl in Boston and New York. Sir, when I came to sea I found the "History of Europe" on the ship's cabin table, the property of the captain; a sort of programme or playbill to tell the seafaring New Englander what he shall find on his landing here. And as for Dombey, sir, there is no land where paper exists to print on where it is not found; no man who can read that does not read it; and if he cannot he finds some charitable pair of eyes that can, and hears it. But these things are not for me to say; these compliments, though true, would better come from one who felt and understand these merits more. I am not here to exchange civilities with you, but rather to speak of that which I am sure interests these gentlemen more than their own praises; of that which is good in holidays and working days, the same in one century and in another century. That which lures a solitary American in the woods with a wish to see England is the moral peculiarity of the Saxon race, its commanding sense of right and wrong, the love and devotion to that—this is the imperial trait which arms them with the sceptre of the globe. It is this which lies at the foundation of that aristocratic character which certainly wanders into strange vagaries, so that its origin is often lost sight of, but which, if it should lose this, would find itself paralysed; and in trade, and in the mechanic's shop, gives that honesty in performance, that thoroughness and solidity of work, which is a national characteristic. This conscience is one element, and the other is that loyal adhesion, that habit of friendship, that homage of man to man, running through all classes—the electing of worthy persons to a certain fraternity, to acts of kindness and warm and staunch support, from year to year, from youth to age, which is alike lovely and honourable to those who render and those who receive it; which stands in strong contrast with the superficial attachments of other races, their excessive courtesy, and short-lived connection. You will think me very pedantic, gentlemen, but, holiday though it be, I have not the smallest interest in any holiday, except as it celebrates real and not pretended joys; and I think it just, in this time of gloom and commercial disaster, of affliction and beggary in these districts, that, on these very accounts I speak of, you should not fail to keep your literary anniversary. I seem to hear you say that, for all that is come and gone yet, we will not reduce by one chaplet or one oak leaf the braveries of our annual feast. For I must tell you, I was given to understand in my childhood, that the British island from which my forefathers came was no lotus garden, no paradise of serene sky and roses, and music and merriment all the year round; no, but a cold, foggy, mournful country, where nothing grew well in the open air, but robust men and virtuous women, and these of a wonderful fibre and endurance; that their best parts were slowly revealed; their virtues did not come out until they quarrelled—they did not strike twelve the first time; good lovers, good haters, and you could know little about them till you had seen them long, and little good of them till you had seen them in action; that in prosperity they were moody and dumpish, but in adversity they were grand. Is it not true, sir, that the wise ancients did not praise the ship parting with flying colours from the port, but only that brave sailer which came back with torn sheets and battered sides, stripped of her banners, but having ridden out the storm? And so, gentlemen, I feel in regard to this aged England, with her possessions, honours, and trophies, and also with the infirmities of a thousand years gathering around her, irretrievably committed as she now is to many old customs which cannot be suddenly changed; pressed upon by the transitions of trade, and new and all incalculable modes, fabrics, arts, machines, and competing populations—I see her not dispirited, not weak, but well remembering that she has seen dark days before; indeed, with a kind of instinct that she sees a little better in a cloudy day, and that in storm of battle and calamity she has a secret vigour and a pulse like a cannon. I see her in her old age, not decrepit, but young, and still daring to believe in her power of endurance and expansion. Seeing this, I say, All hail! mother of nations, mother of heroes, with strength still equal to the time; still wise to entertain and swift to execute the policy which the mind and heart of mankind requires in the present hour, and thus only hospitable to the foreigner, and truly a home to the thoughtful and generous who are born in the soil. So be it! so let it be. If it be not so, if the courage of England goes with the chances of a commercial crisis, I will go back to the capes of Massachusetts, and my own Indian stream, and say to my own countrymen, the old race are all gone, and the elasticity and hope of mankind must henceforth remain on the Alleghany ranges, or nowhere.

ARTICLES ON EMERSON AND HIS WRITINGS IN THE ENGLISH AND AMERICAN PERIODICALS.

EMERSON, R. W. (R. Buchanan) Broadway, 2 : 223.—(J. Burroughs) Galaxy, 21 : 254, 543.—(Delia M. Colton) Continental Monthly, 1 : 49.—(G. Gilfillan) Tait's Magazine, New Series, 15 : 17.—(J. O'Connor) Catholic World, 27 : 90.—(G. Prentice) Methodist Quarterly, 24 : 357.—Dublin Review, 26 : 152.—North British Review, 47 : 319.—Westminster Review, 33 : 345.—Same art., Living Age, 16 : 97.—Blackwood, 62 : 643.—(F. H. Underwood) North American Review, 130 : 485.

—— *Address, July, 1838.* Boston Quarterly, 1 : 500.
—— *Address on Forefather's Day.* (I. N. Tarbox) New Englander, 30 : 175.
—— *and his Writings.* (G. Barmby) Howitt's Journal, 2 : 315.—Christian Review, 26 : 640.
—— *and History.* Southern Literary Messenger, 18 : 249.
—— *and Landor.* Living Age, 52 : 371.
—— *and the Pantheists.* (H. Hemming) New Dominion Monthly, 8 : 65.
—— *and Transcendentalism.* American Whig Review, 1 : 233.
—— *and Spencer and Martineau.* (W. R. Alger) Christian Examiner, 84 : 257.
—— *Conduct of Life.* (N. Porter) New Englander, 19 : 496.—Eclectic Review, 46 : 365.
—— *Culture of.* Fraser, 78 : 1. Same art., Living Age, 98 : 358.
—— *Essays.* Democratic Review, 16 : 589.—Eclectic Magazine, 18 : 546.— Living Age, 4 : 139; 23 : 344.—(C. C. Felton) Christian Examiner, 30 : 252.— Eclectic Review, 76 : 667.—Boston Quarterly, 4 : 391.—Biblical Review, 1 : 148.—Eclectic Review, 76 : 667.—Prospective Review, 1 : 232.—Tait's Magazine, new series, 8 : 666.
—— *Facts about.* Chambers' Journal, 21 : 382.
—— *Homes and Haunts of.* (F. B. Sanborn) Scribner, 17 : 496.
—— *Lectures at Manchester, England.* Howitt's Journal, 2 : 370.
—— *Lectures and Writings of.* Every Saturday, 3 : 680 ; 4 : 381.
—— *Letters and Social Aims.* International Review, 3 : 249.
—— *New Lectures.* New Englander, 8 : 166.—Christian Review, 15 : 249.
—— *Poems of.* (C. E. Norton) Nation, 4 : 430.—American Whig Review, 6 : 197.—(C. A. Bartol) Christian Examiner, 42 : 250.—Southern Literary Messenger, 13 : 292.—Brownson, 4 : 262.—Democratic Review, 1 : 319.— Christian Remembrancer, 15 : 300.
—— *Prose Works.* Catholic World, 11 : 202.
—— *Recent Lectures and Writings.* Fraser, 75 : 586.—Same art., Living Age, 93 : 581.

EMERSON, R. W. *Representative Men.* (C. A. Bartol) Christian Examiner, 48 : 314.—Eclectic Review, 95 : 568.—British Quarterly, 11 : 281.

——— *Society and Solitude.* Fraser, 82 : 1.

——— *Writings.* (F. H. Hedge) Christian Examiner, 38 : 87.—(J. W. Alexander) Princeton Review, 13 : 539.

FOREIGN TRANSLATIONS OF, AND ARTICLES ON, EMERSON.

Edgar Quinet, in a volume of Lectures on "Christianity and the French Revolution," 1845, devotes one to "America and the Reformation," in which he thus expresses his opinion of Emerson:—"In this North America, which is pictured to us as so materialistic, I find the most ideal writer of our times. Contrast the formulas of German Philosophy with the inspiration, the initiative, the moral *élan* of Emerson. The author I have just named is proof enough that bold pioneers are at work in America pursuing the quest of truth in the moral world. What we announce in Europe from the summit of a revived past, he also announces from the germinating solitude of a world absolutely new. On the virgin soil of the new world behold the footsteps of a man, and a man who is moving toward the future by the same road that we are going."

In the "Revue Independante," 1846, the Countess D'Agoult, under her pseudonym of "Daniel Stern," has an article on "The Literary Tendencies of America," in which Emerson is highly appreciated. Philarète Chasles also wrote about him.

Emile Montégut, in the "Revue des Deux Mondes," has written on Emerson in an article entitled "An American Thinker and Poet," 1847. "Hero Worship : Emerson and Carlyle," 1850. "English Character judged by an American," 1856.

Herman Grimm, in 1857, published a translation of Emerson's "Goethe" and "Shakespeare" in "Representative Men," with a criticism on his writings. Some sentences from this criticism, as well as from another work by the same author, "New Essays," will be found at page 36, "Memoir."

H. Wolff gives a life of Emerson in a Dutch work, published at Bois le Duc, 1871, entitled "Prophets of Modern Date."

www.ingramcontent.com/pod-product-compliance
Lightning Source LLC
Chambersburg PA
CBHW020133170426
43199CB00010B/731